Words of Light
نور الكلمات

Paintings and Reflections
by Dr. Lamaat Shalaby

ISBN 978-1-959536-12-3 (Hardcover)
ISBN 978-1-959536-13-0 (Paperback)

First edition 2025

Published by Honey Elm Books LLC
www.HoneyElmBooks.com

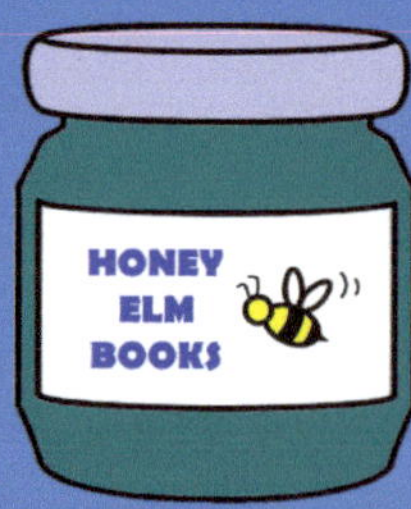

DEDICATION

To Allah, the ONE and Most Compassionate. In appreciation of His many blessings.

To everyone who is reading my book.

CONTENTS

NOTES and REFERENCES:

****

ACKNOWLEDGEMENTS

To the team who initiated and worked hard to make this book a reality:

Noha, my niece, Dr. Zeinab and Dr. Wafaa, my sisters,

Dr. Magid, my husband, Dr. El Mouelhi, my brother-in-law, and Dr. Haleem, a dear friend.

To my parents' memory for showing me the way to the Noor.

- Lamaat Shalaby

ABOUT THE AUTHOR

Dr. Lamaat Shalaby was born in Egypt. Her parents emphasized Islamic values in her upbringing. She received a Bachelor's degree in Pharmacy from Cairo University. She moved to the United States with her husband to pursue graduate degrees for both of them. She received her Doctorate degree in the United States. Being a scientist, she always appreciated Allah's (SWT) creations.

Dr. Shalaby showed true talent in drawing and painting early on, but took a break for a while to focus on family and career. Her daughter gifted her with a watercolor set, and this thoughtful gesture reignited her joy for painting. She started a wonderful collection of paintings with Qur'anic verses, combining her talent with her appreciation of Allah's (SWT) blessings.

Her niece started this wonderful idea to publish her collection and asked her to write some commentary to accompany each painting. And this is when all the magic happened. Dr. Shalaby wrote beautiful comments to share with others in this book.

We hope the readers will enjoy both her paintings and her writing.

May Allah (SWT) reward her and accept her work.

- The Editors

INTRODUCTION

Growing up, I was always fascinated with nature. I felt there was something special about it that made me feel at ease. I used to watch the sunrises from behind the Mokattam Hills in Cairo, Egypt, and the sunsets behind the Pyramids. I remember observing the beauty of the giant red Canna blossoms and comparing them with the delicate scented Jasmine flowers that my father had planted.

As a young child, I remember watching my father reading big, heavy reference books and writing manuscripts in all his spare time. My father was a scholar and an author of numerous books in Islamic studies. I used to think that all fathers were like my father.

As I got older, I started to appreciate the depth of my father's knowledge and his strong belief and commitment to Allah (SWT). I started an ongoing dialogue with my father to learn more about important subjects, such as who created the universe and why are we on earth? My father would answer my questions with an encouraging smile and say, " Oh, my child, I have searched in all kinds of man-written books to answer those questions and I found the truth only in Allah's Holy Book, The Qur'an" .

My love of nature and the appreciation of the miraculous creation of Allah Ta'ala helped me to discover painting as a hobby. I found it was a way for me to express the beauty and wisdom in Allah's creations.

Over the years I have drawn numerous watercolor paintings covering many subjects, but I especially loved nature. In the spring of 2023, I started to add Qur'anic verses which I would recite to calm my heart.

{ Those who believe and whose hearts find comfort in the remembrance of Allah. Surely in the remembrance of Allah do hearts find comfort. } Ar-Ra'd-28

Then I added more and more of the Qur'an — "Words of Light".

This is how this art collection has come about, and I will share more with you as we go through this book.

- Lamaat Shalaby

Paintings
and
Reflections

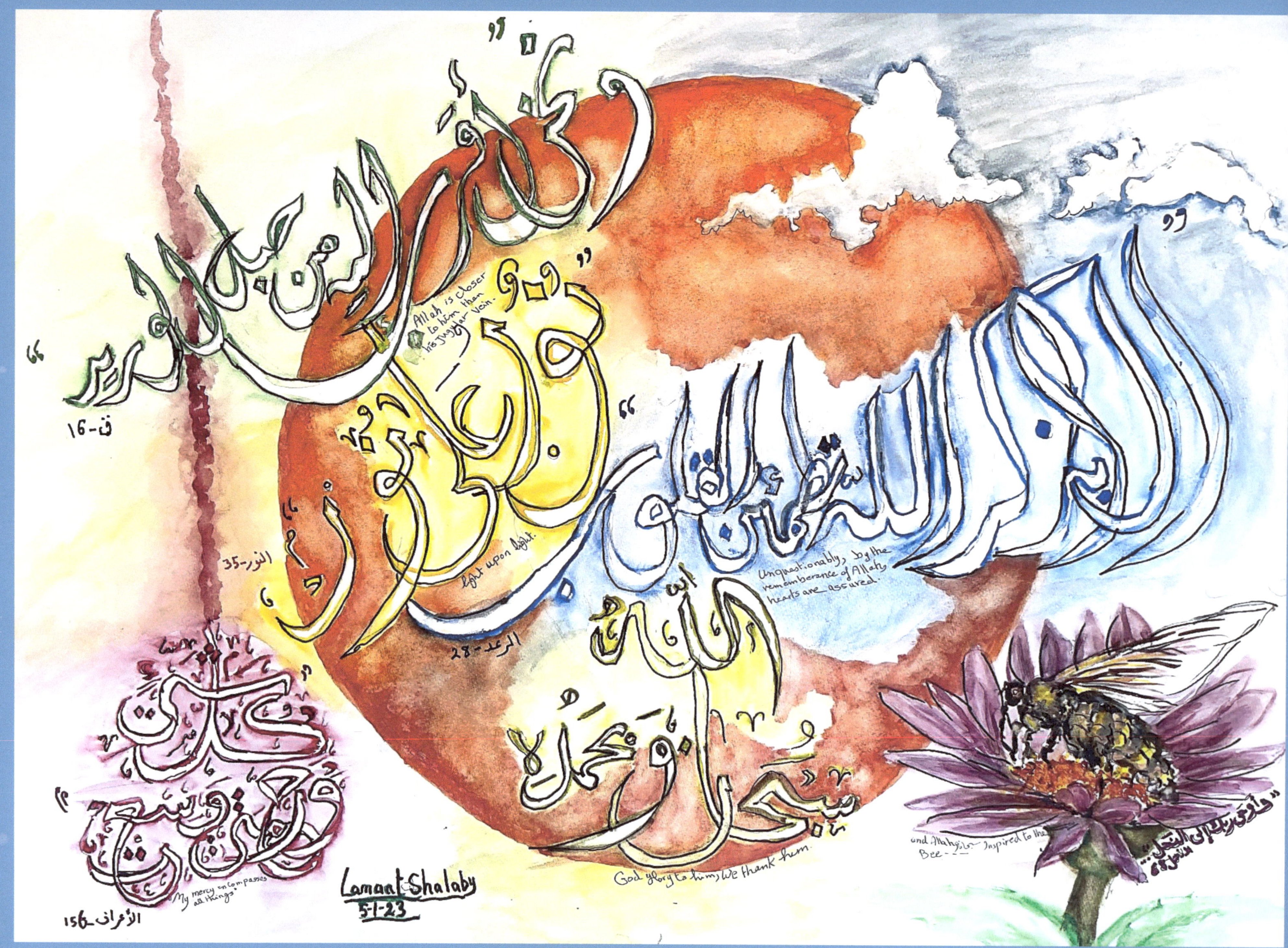

Allah is closer to him than His Jugular Vein.
Light upon light.
Unquestionably, by the remembrance of Allah hearts are assured.
My mercy encompasses all things
God glory to him, We thank him.
and thy Lord Inspired to the Bee —
Lamaat Shalaby
5-1-23

Hearts at Peace

I was reading the Qur'an and stopped at the verses where Allah, glory to Him, mentions that He is closer to us than our body's major vein. I felt self-conscious… am I worth this huge gift and responsibility? I also felt that I am accountable for my choices.

{ We created man -- We know the promptings of his soul, and we are closer to him than his jugular vein –} **Qaf-16**

Then when I read the second verse that says that remembering Allah and reciting his words will bring calmness to our hearts, I was relieved and hopeful.

{ Those who believe and whose hearts find comfort in the remembrance of God -- surely in the remembrance of God hearts can find comfort.} Ar-Ra'd-28

Allah, glory to Him, said that His Mercy embraces everything in the Universe.

{ Grant us good things, both in this life and in the hereafter. To You alone we turn. He replied, As for My punishment, I smite anyone I will. But My mercy encompasses all things. I shall prescribe it for those who do their duty, pay the zakat and who believe in Our signs.} **Al-A'raf-156**

…………………………………………

Other Qur'anic Verses in the Painting:

{ God is the light of the heavens and the earth. His light may be compared to a niche containing a lamp, the lamp inside a crystal of star-like brilliance lit from a blessed olive tree, neither of the east nor of the west. The [luminous] oil is as if ready to burn without even touching it. Light upon Light; God guides to His light whom He will. God draws such comparisons for mankind; God has full knowledge of everything.} **An-Noor-35**

{ Your Lord inspired the bee, saying, "Make your homes in the mountains, in the trees, and also in the structures which men erect.} **An-Nahl-68**

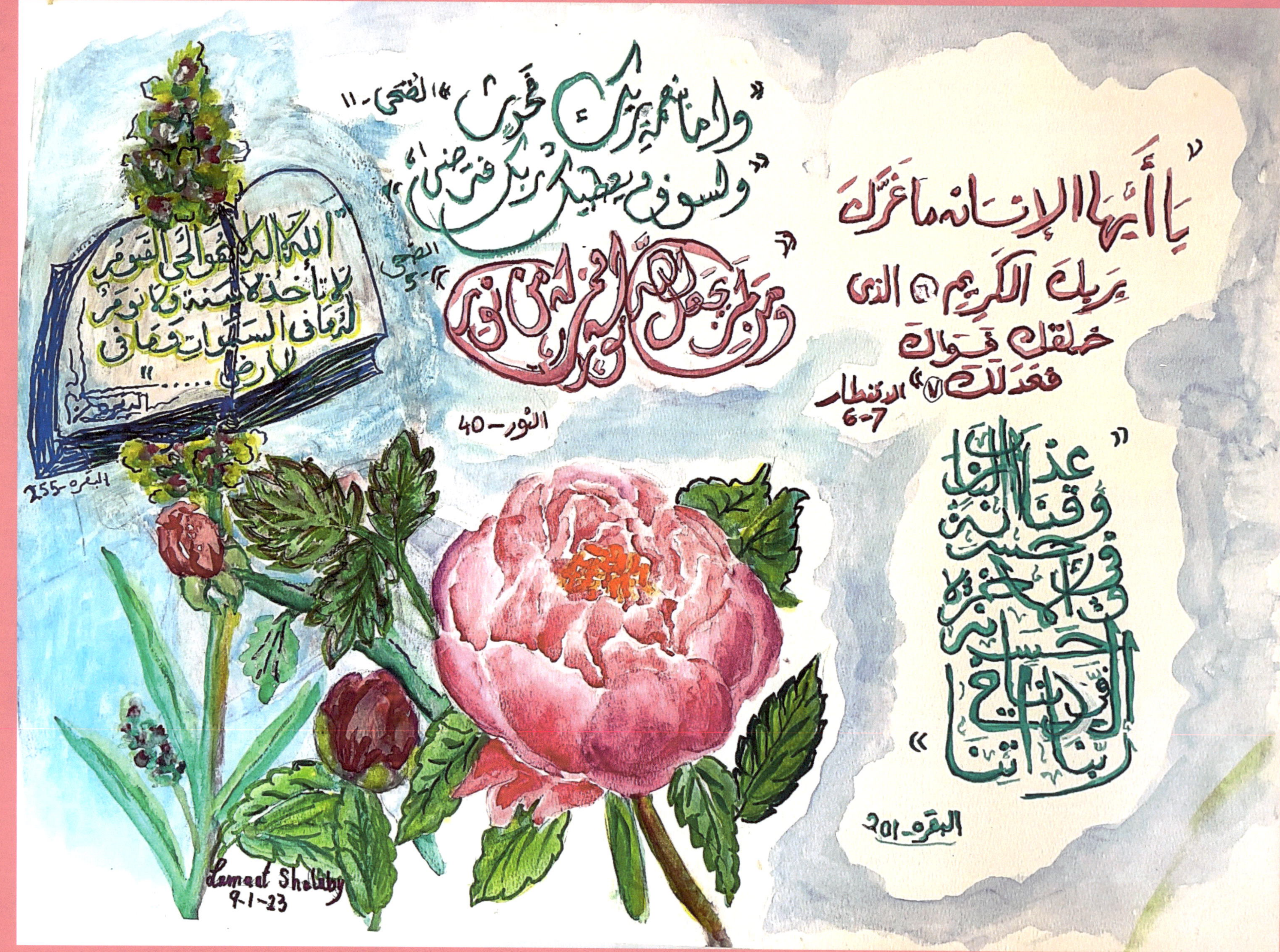

وَالَّمَاءُ وَمَا بَنَاهَا
«الشمس - ١١»
وَلَسَوْفَ يُعْطِيكَ رَبُّكَ فَتَرْضَى
«الضحى»
يَا أَيُّهَا الْإِنْسَانُ مَا غَرَّكَ بِرَبِّكَ الْكَرِيمِ ٦ الَّذِي خَلَقَكَ فَسَوَّاكَ فَعَدَلَكَ ٧
«الإنفطار ٦-٧»
اللَّهُ لَا إِلَهَ إِلَّا هُوَ الْحَيُّ الْقَيُّومُ لَا تَأْخُذُهُ سِنَةٌ وَلَا نَوْمٌ لَهُ مَا فِي السَّمَاوَاتِ وَمَا فِي الْأَرْضِ
«البقرة - ٢٥٥»
وَمَن لَّمْ يَجْعَلِ اللَّهُ لَهُ نُورًا فَمَا لَهُ مِن نُورٍ
«النور - ٤٥»
وَقِنَا عَذَابَ النَّارِ
«البقرة - ٢٠١»
Lamaa Sholby
9-1-23

Allah, The Sustainer of All that Exists

I was drawing these beautiful roses and thanking Allah, the Creator for His Grace. I felt a desire to write verses of the Holy Qur'an to recite whenever I looked at the painting. This is how I started this painting album.

Every day when I wake up early to pray Fajr, I open the window to smell the fresh air and enjoy the calmness of the dawn and its tranquility. As I recite the verse of Al-Korsy (The Throne) in Surah Al-Baqara where it describes that Allah, the Almighty, does not sleep nor take naps, I thank Him for overseeing the world - day and night - while we are asleep.

{ Allah: there is no deity except Him, the Living, the Eternal One. Neither slumber nor sleep overtakes Him. To Him belong whatsoever is in the heavens and whatsoever is on the earth. Who can intercede with Him except by His permission? He knows all that is before them and all that is behind them. They can grasp only that part of His knowledge which He wills. His throne extends over the heavens and the earth; and their upholding does not weary Him. He is the Sublime, the Almighty One! } Al-Baqara-255

....

Other Qur'anic Verses in the Painting:

{ Soon you will be gratified with what your Lord will give you. } Adh-Dhuha-5

{ And proclaim the blessings of your Lord. } Adh-Dhuha-11

{ Or [the state of a disbeliever] is like darkness on a deep ocean covered by waves billowing over waves and overcast with clouds: darkness upon darkness. If he stretches out his hand, he can scarcely see it. Indeed, the man from whom God withholds His light shall find no light at all. }
An-Noor-40

{ And there are others who pray, "Our Lord, grant us good in this world as well as good in the Hereafter, and protect us from the torment of the Fire." } Al-Baqara-201

{ O man! What is it that lures you away from your bountiful Sustainer, (6) who created you, fashioned you and proportioned you, (7) }
Al-Infitar-6&7

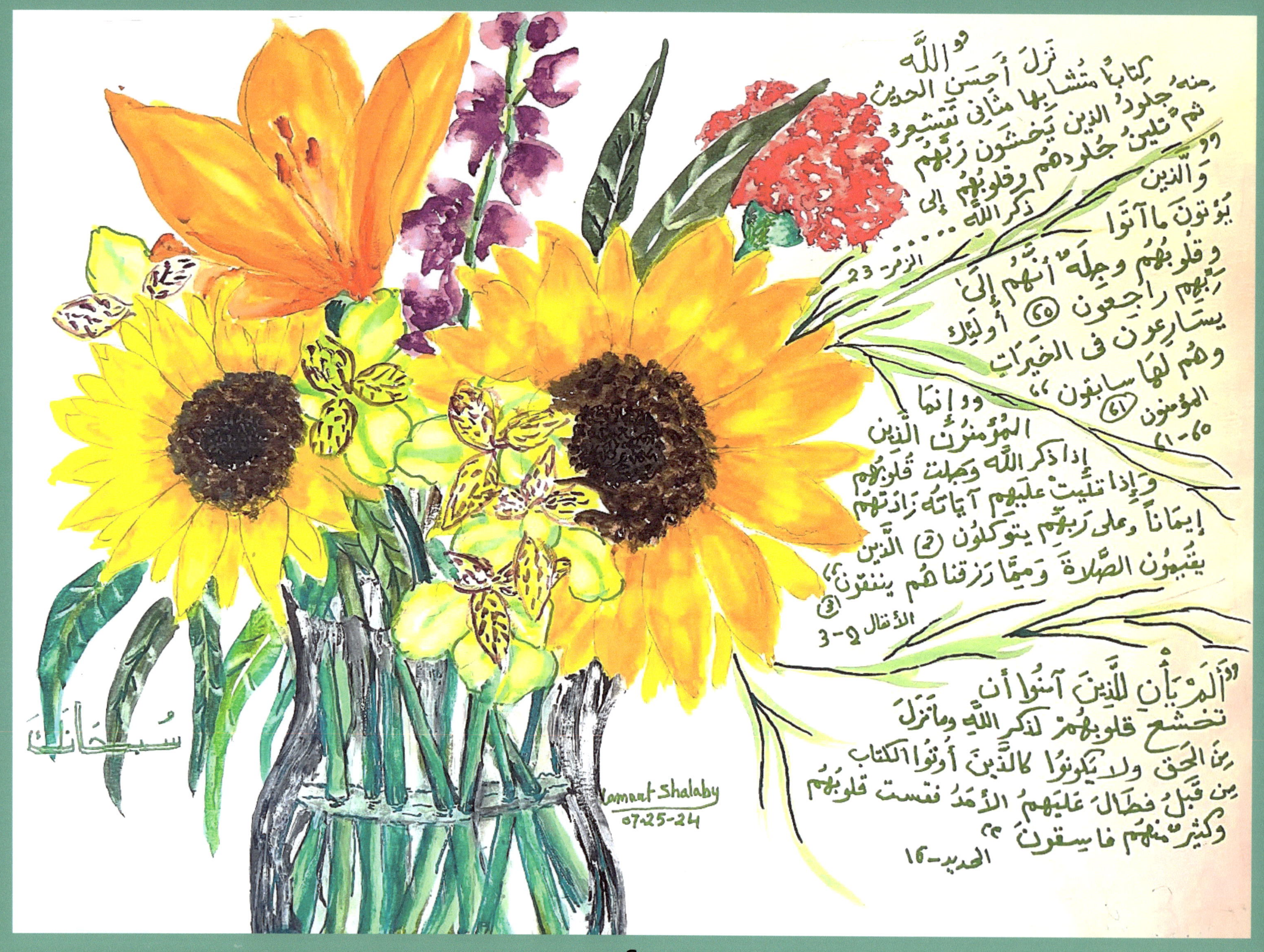

اللَّهُ نَزَّلَ أَحْسَنَ الْحَدِيثِ كِتَابًا مُتَشَابِهًا مَثَانِيَ تَقْشَعِرُّ مِنْهُ جُلُودُ الَّذِينَ يَخْشَوْنَ رَبَّهُمْ ثُمَّ تَلِينُ جُلُودُهُمْ وَقُلُوبُهُمْ إِلَى ذِكْرِ اللَّهِ
الزمر - ٢٣
وَالَّذِينَ يُؤْتُونَ مَا آتَوْا وَقُلُوبُهُمْ وَجِلَةٌ أَنَّهُمْ إِلَى رَبِّهِمْ رَاجِعُونَ ۝ أُولَٰئِكَ يُسَارِعُونَ فِي الْخَيْرَاتِ وَهُمْ لَهَا سَابِقُونَ ۝
المؤمنون ٦٠ - ٦١
إِنَّمَا الْمُؤْمِنُونَ الَّذِينَ إِذَا ذُكِرَ اللَّهُ وَجِلَتْ قُلُوبُهُمْ وَإِذَا تُلِيَتْ عَلَيْهِمْ آيَاتُهُ زَادَتْهُمْ إِيمَانًا وَعَلَىٰ رَبِّهِمْ يَتَوَكَّلُونَ ۝ الَّذِينَ يُقِيمُونَ الصَّلَاةَ وَمِمَّا رَزَقْنَاهُمْ يُنْفِقُونَ ۝
الأنفال ٢ - ٣
أَلَمْ يَأْنِ لِلَّذِينَ آمَنُوا أَنْ تَخْشَعَ قُلُوبُهُمْ لِذِكْرِ اللَّهِ وَمَا نَزَلَ مِنَ الْحَقِّ وَلَا يَكُونُوا كَالَّذِينَ أُوتُوا الْكِتَابَ مِنْ قَبْلُ فَطَالَ عَلَيْهِمُ الْأَمَدُ فَقَسَتْ قُلُوبُهُمْ وَكَثِيرٌ مِنْهُمْ فَاسِقُونَ ۝
الحديد - ١٦
سُبْحَانَكَ

The Qur'an is the Authentic Word from Allah

Allah Almighty described the Qur'an as the best hadith. It is the Truth. Most of what is written by man nowadays is not the whole truth and is done for a certain self-serving purpose. If a person writes about the truth, he is held accountable. And had it not been for the Book of Allah Almighty as the source of the truth and guidance, mankind would have lost its way.

One of the miracles of the Holy Qur'an is that it is the only book that people do not get tired of reading repeatedly. It is the words of Allah Almighty that guide hearts to the straight path, the light of faith and tranquility. It is the path to success in this world and the Paradise that Allah promised the believers.

{ Allah has revealed (from time to time) the most beautiful Message in the form of a Book, consistent with itself, (Yet) repeating (its teaching in various aspects): the skins of those who fear their Lord tremble thereat; then their skins and their hearts do soften to the celebration of Allah's praises. Such is the guidance of Allah: He guides therewith whom He pleases, but such as Allah leaves to stray, can have none to guide. }
Az-Zumar-23

The Holy Qur'an is a gift from Allah Almighty to His servants to bring them out of the darkness of disbelief and disobedience to the light of faith and reward. The Qur'an's verses confirm that the message of all prophets is the same, which is that Allah is One and the Creator of the universe with wisdom and control. Mankind is to worship Him, the One and Only, and follow His guidance to be rewarded Paradise.

Allah describes the believers with an accurate description in the Qur'an that if they receive something, they feel guilty to use it. This feeling is close to my heart.

{ and those who give to others what has been bestowed upon them with their hearts trembling at the thought that they must return to their Lord; (60) it is they who vie with one another in doing good works and shall be the foremost in doing so. (61) }
Al-Mu'menoon-60&61

The believer fears Allah, and when he hears Allah's name, it assures his faith, and he leans on Allah. The believer establishes prayers and spends for the sake of Allah.

[True believers are those whose hearts tremble with awe at the mention of God, and whose faith grows stronger as they listen to His revelations. They are those who put their trust in their Lord, (2) who pray regularly and give in alms out of what We have provided for them. (3) }
Al-Anfal-2&3

Allah reminds the believers that their hearts should always turn to the remembrance of Allah and what has been revealed to them. And not to be like the people of the book who forgot their religion as time went by.

{ Has the time not come for the faithful when their hearts in all humility should engage in the remembrance of God and of the revelation of truth, so that they should not become like those who were given the Book before them, whose hearts with the passage of time became hardened and many of whom were disobedient?} Al-Hadid-16

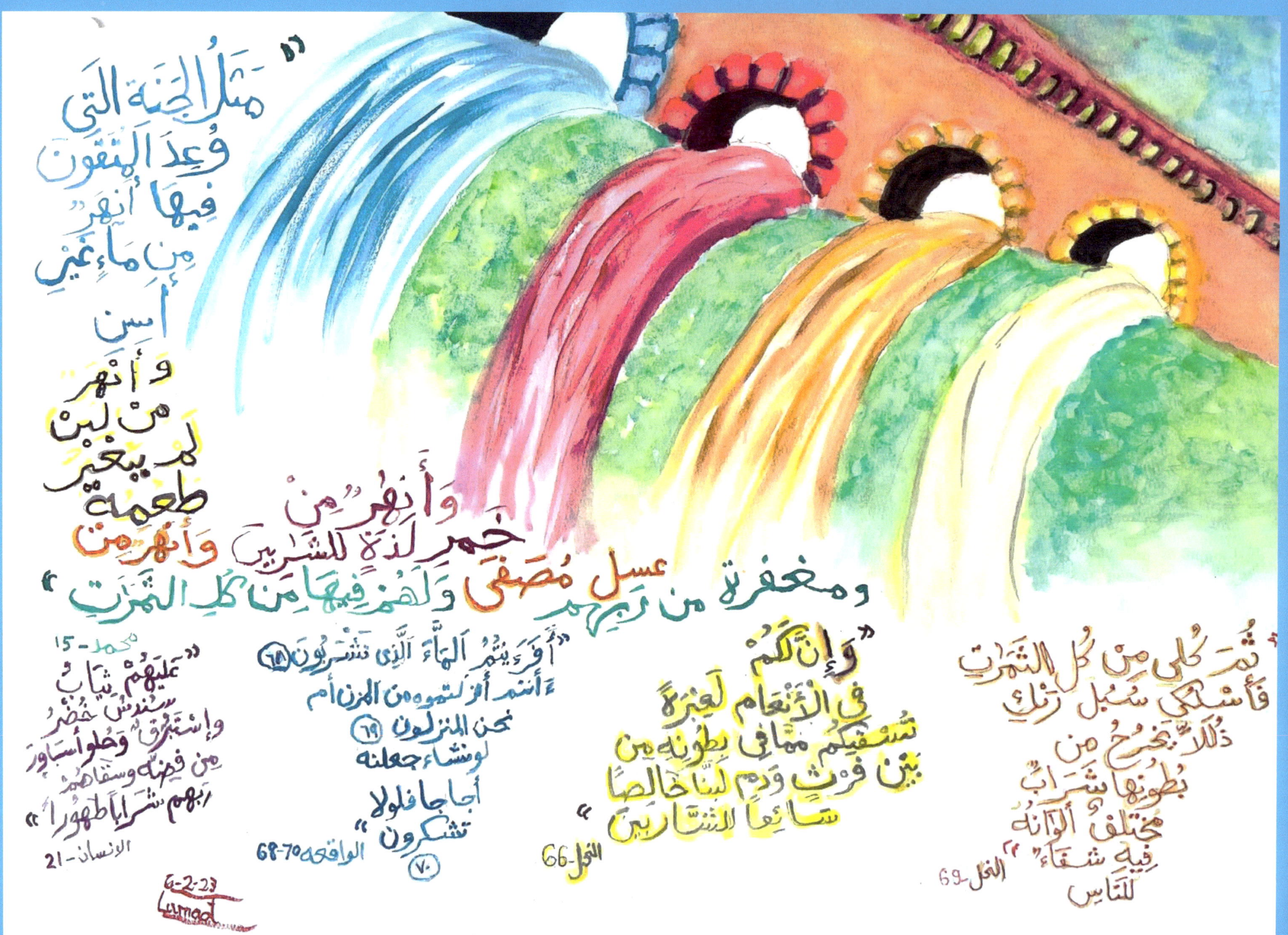
"مَثَلُ الْجَنَّةِ الَّتِي وُعِدَ الْمُتَّقُونَ فِيهَا أَنْهَارٌ مِنْ مَاءٍ غَيْرِ آسِنٍ وَأَنْهَارٌ مِنْ لَبَنٍ لَمْ يَتَغَيَّرْ طَعْمُهُ وَأَنْهَارٌ مِنْ خَمْرٍ لَذَّةٍ لِلشَّارِبِينَ وَأَنْهَارٌ مِنْ عَسَلٍ مُصَفًّى وَلَهُمْ فِيهَا مِنْ كُلِّ الثَّمَرَاتِ وَمَغْفِرَةٌ مِنْ رَبِّهِمْ"
محمد - 15

"عَالِيَهُمْ ثِيَابُ سُنْدُسٍ خُضْرٌ وَإِسْتَبْرَقٌ وَحُلُّوا أَسَاوِرَ مِنْ فِضَّةٍ وَسَقَاهُمْ رَبُّهُمْ شَرَابًا طَهُورًا"
الإنسان - 21

"أَفَرَأَيْتُمُ الْمَاءَ الَّذِي تَشْرَبُونَ ۝ أَأَنْتُمْ أَنْزَلْتُمُوهُ مِنَ الْمُزْنِ أَمْ نَحْنُ الْمُنْزِلُونَ ۝ لَوْ نَشَاءُ جَعَلْنَاهُ أُجَاجًا فَلَوْلَا تَشْكُرُونَ ۝"
الواقعة 68-70

"وَإِنَّ لَكُمْ فِي الْأَنْعَامِ لَعِبْرَةً نُسْقِيكُمْ مِمَّا فِي بُطُونِهِ مِنْ بَيْنِ فَرْثٍ وَدَمٍ لَبَنًا خَالِصًا سَائِغًا لِلشَّارِبِينَ"
النحل 66

"ثُمَّ كُلِي مِنْ كُلِّ الثَّمَرَاتِ فَاسْلُكِي سُبُلَ رَبِّكِ ذُلُلًا يَخْرُجُ مِنْ بُطُونِهَا شَرَابٌ مُخْتَلِفٌ أَلْوَانُهُ فِيهِ شِفَاءٌ لِلنَّاسِ"
النحل 69

The Rivers of Jannah

How beautiful it is to think about Allah Almighty's description in the Qur'an of His beautiful Paradise. I stopped when I was reading His Majesty describing the rivers in Heaven. There are four kinds of rivers - one of pure water, one of fresh milk, one of tasty wine which does not make you drunk, and one of pure honey. That is what we wish for and strive to achieve in our lives by obeying Allah Almighty.

{ Here is a description of the Garden promised to the righteous: therein are rivers of water which is forever pure; and rivers of milk of which the taste never changes; and rivers of wine, a delight to those who drink it, and rivers of pure honey. And in it they will have all kinds of fruit, and will receive forgiveness from their Lord… } Muhammad-15

Then I tried to understand the Wisdom in creating each of these four liquids that provide us with both our needs and pleasure.

Water is such a vital liquid that no life can exist without it. This miraculous liquid was created by Allah from two hydrogen atoms and one oxygen atom. This composition gives water all its qualities and characteristics. It has no color or taste. The sun's heat induces evaporation of sea water to form clouds, then comes the rain, the rivers and springs and so on, in what we now know as the vital water cycle. It is amazing how water evaporates from the salty oceans and turns into fresh water, leaving behind the salt. This water serves mankind, animals, and plants. Glory be to Allah and His perfect creation.

{ Have you considered the water that you drink? (68) Is it you who caused it to descend from the clouds, or did We? (69) If we were so pleased, We certainly could make it salty. Why, then, are you not grateful? (70) } Al-Waqi'a-68-70

The rivers of milk in heaven do not get spoiled nor need to be cooled, and this is Allah's gift. The milk that we drink while being on earth, Allah Almighty created it pure, white, and tasty, even though it originated from the animal's udder and between blood and excretions.

{ There is also a lesson for you in cattle. From the contents of their bellies, from between the dung and blood, We give you pure milk to drink, pleasant for those who drink it. } An-Nahl-66

The wine in Heaven is tasty but does not make you drunk, in contrast to wine on earth.

{ They will wear green garments of fine silk and rich brocade. They will be adorned with silver bracelets. And their Lord will give them a pure drink. } Al-Insan-21

And honey was created by the inspiration from Allah to the bees to absorb the nectar of flowers and with their special digestive system can make honey and store it to feed their offspring and as food and medicine for mankind.

{ Then [Bees] feed on every kind of fruit, and follow the trodden paths of your Lord." From its belly comes a drink with different colors which provides healing for mankind. Indeed, in this there is a sign for people who give thought. } An-Nahl-69

Human research continues to develop and progress. We are slowly learning about the wisdom of Allah's creations. When mankind's discoveries reach the real truth, we will gain a deeper understanding of many of the verses in the Qur'an revealed over 1400 years ago.

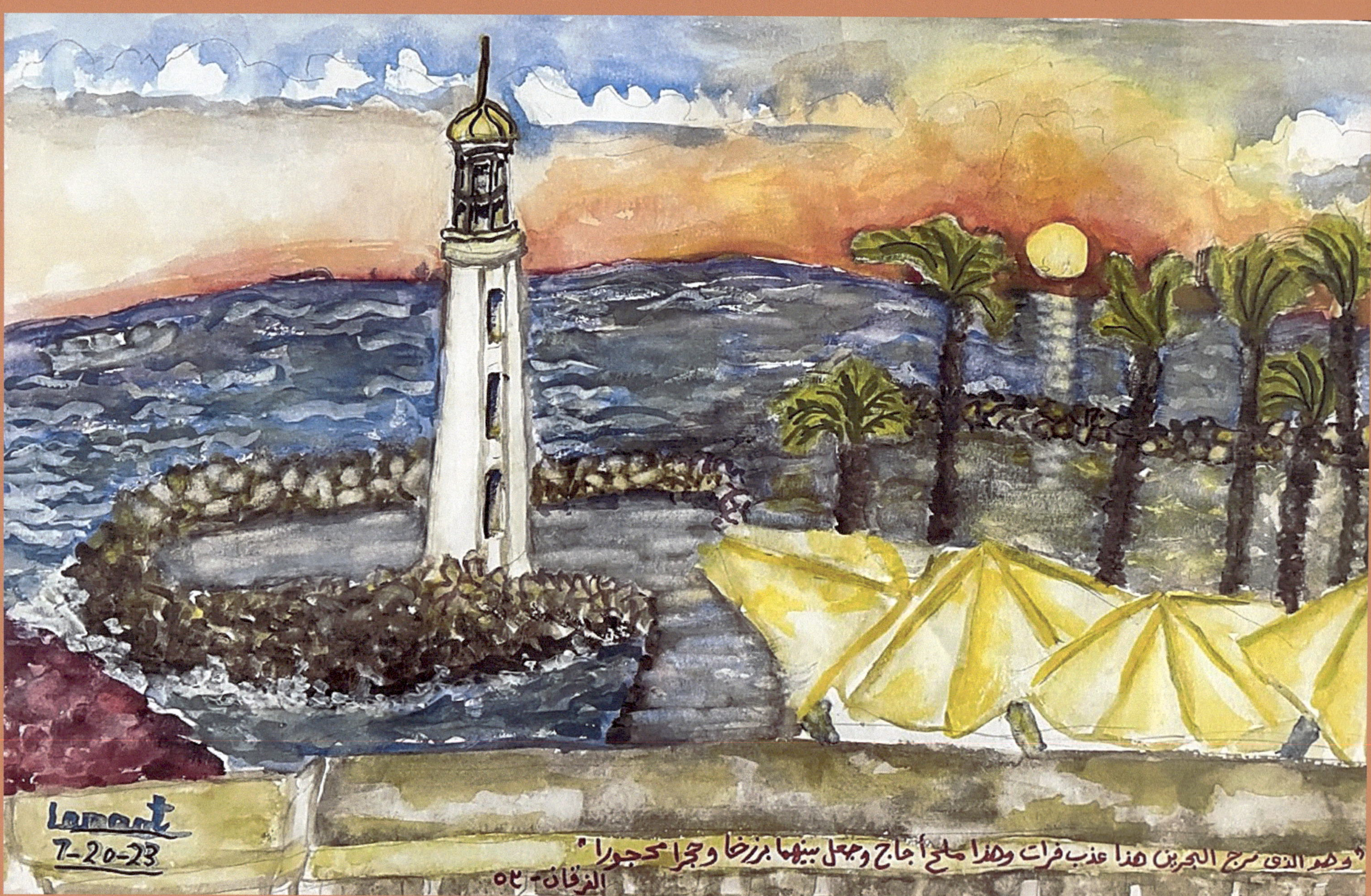
وهو الذي مرج البحرين هذا عذب فرات وهذا ملح أجاج وجعل بينهما برزخا وحجرا محجورا
الفرقان - ٥٣
Lamant
7-20-23

The Strait between the River and the Sea

How beautiful are the creations of Allah Almighty and His miraculous Wisdom. This is the sunrise in the city of Ras al-Bar in Egypt, where the Damietta branch of the River Nile pours into the Mediterranean Sea. I can see the barrier behind the palm trees , an abrupt color change between the Nile water that tends to be brown from the Nile silt and the blue sea water with its waves. It is the wisdom of Allah Almighty that He created this chemical and geographic barrier so that the saltwater of the sea does not overwhelm the freshwater of the rivers.

{ It is He who released the two bodies of flowing water, one sweet and fresh and the other salty and bitter, and set up an insurmountable barrier between them. } Al-Forqan-53

Nowadays, mankind due to his ignorance and injustice has tampered with the environment and the divine laws on earth. And the harmful effects appear in all aspects of life. Look at the words of Allah Almighty:

{ Corruption has appeared on land and sea because of the evil which the hands of men have done: and so He [Allah] will make them taste the fruit of some of their doings, so that they may turn back from evil. } Ar-Room-41

In a few enlightening words from Allah, He informed us in the Qur'an over 1400 years ago what would happen. Allah also informed us that mankind will suffer from the damage he caused and this will force him to reform it by following the divine laws.

Glory be to Allah, He has mercy on mankind despite mankind's sins against the universe because of his ego and greed. Allah Almighty gives mankind opportunities to fix his mistakes. He is the most Merciful and most Wise.

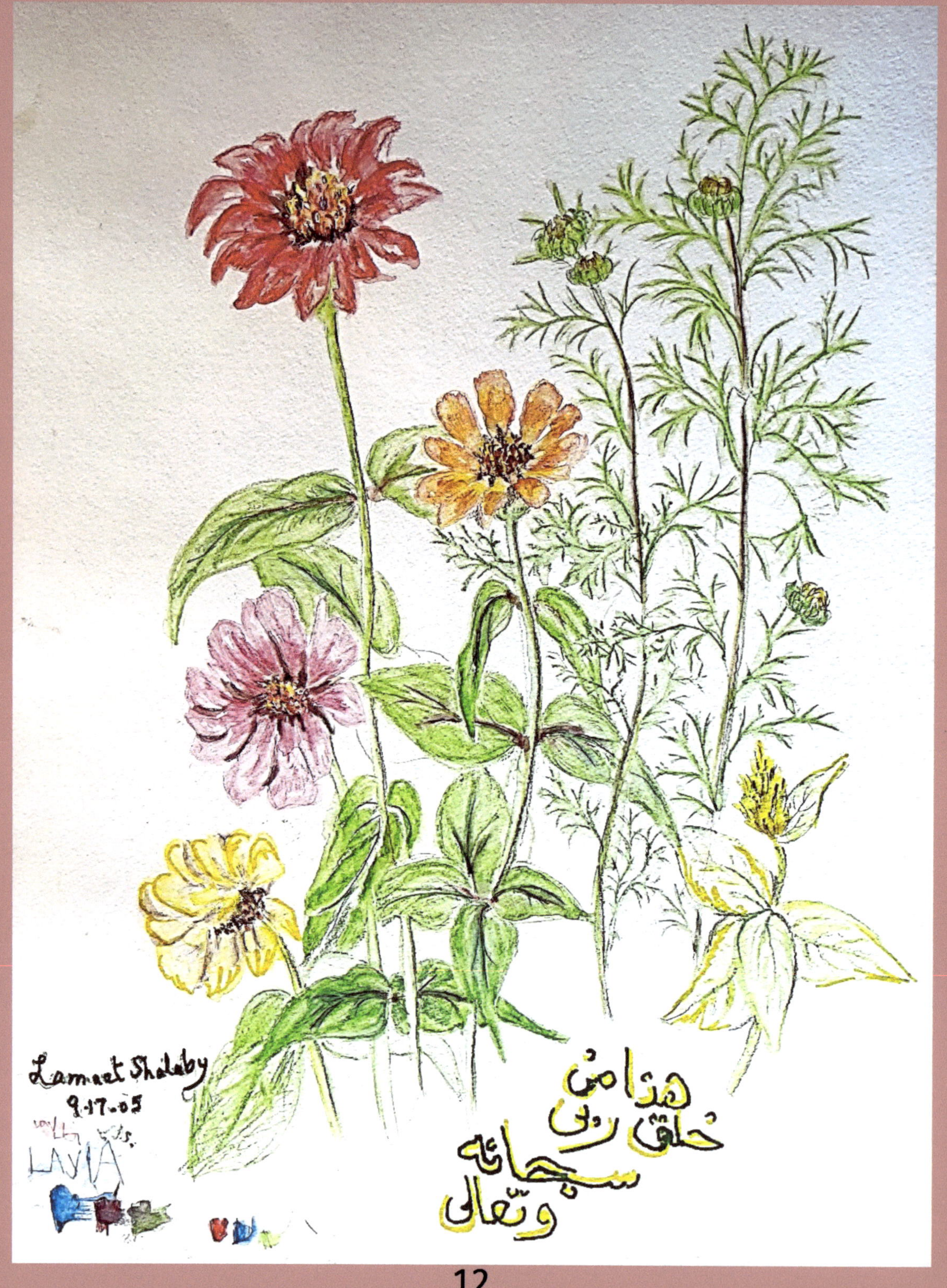

Lamaat Shalaby
9-17-05
هذا من
خلق ربي
سبحانه
وتعالى

Layla's Flower

This painting is nineteen-years-old. It was drawn with watercolor pencils. It is of special value to me because my then five-year-old granddaughter, Layla, joined me in drawing it and signed her name and added some hearts. Grandchildren are a blessing from Allah, the All Merciful, to me.

{ God has given you wives from among yourselves, and given you children and grandchildren from your wives, and provided wholesome things for you. Will they then believe in falsehood and deny God's favors? } An-Nahl-72

One of the great blessings from Allah Ta'ala, is what was mentioned in verse 96 of Surah Maryam.

{ The Lord of Mercy will bestow affection upon those who believe and perform righteous deeds. } Maryam-96

And in the hadith too:

(When God loves a believer, God calls Gabriel and says: God loves so-and-so, so love him, and Gabriel will love him. Then Gabriel calls out the dwellers of heaven: God loves so-and-so, so love him, so the dwellers of heaven will love him, and then acceptance is placed for him on earth. And if Allah hates a person, He calls Gabriel and says: I hate so-and-so, so hate him. Gabriel will hate him. Then Gabriel calls out the dwellers of heaven: God hates so-and-so, so hate him, and the dwellers of heaven will hate him and then hatred is placed for him on earth.)

Narrated by Abu Hurayrah in Sahih Al-Bukhari

This affection means that Allah's love spreads love to all creatures of the universe, and we should strive to earn it.

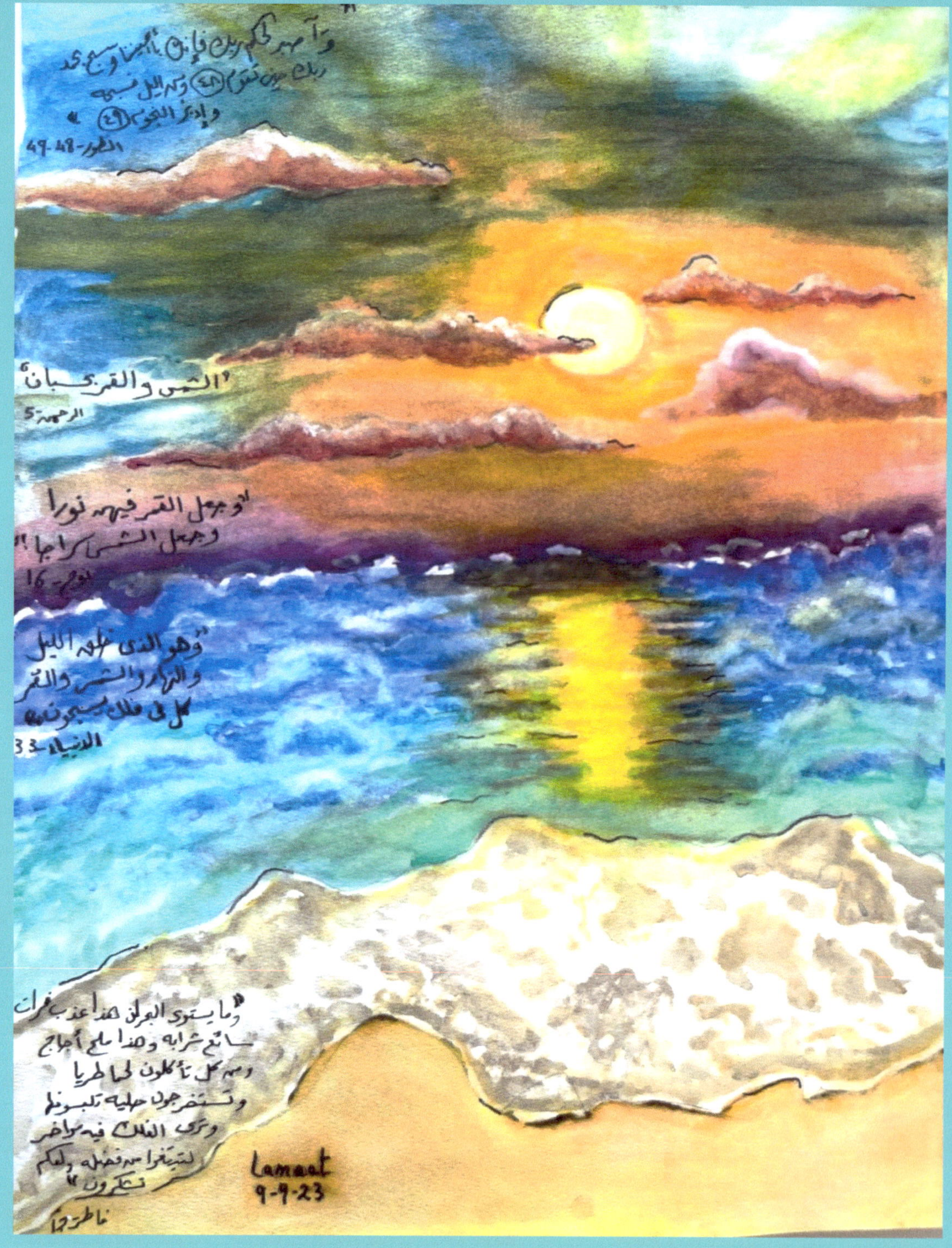
وَآمِنُوا بِاللَّهِ وَرَسُولِهِ
الطور - 48-49

"الشمس والقربان"
الرحمن 5

"وجعل القمر فيهن نورا
وجعل الشمس سراجا"
نوح - 16

"وهو الذي خلق الليل
والنهار والشمس والقمر
كل في فلك يسبحون"
الأنبياء - 33

Lamaat
9-9-23

فاطر

The Sun and the Moon

The sunset and its reflection on the surface of the sea is one of Allah's beautiful creations. We thank Allah for creating the sun to warm us with its heat and to provide plants with the energy necessary to generate food through the process of photosynthesis. This vital process requires sunlight and uses carbon dioxide which is generated from our exhalation and in return provides us with the oxygen necessary for our breathing.

In these chosen verses, Allah Almighty reminds us of many signs of His creations. The creation of the sun, the moon, the day, and the night.

{ The sun and the moon move according to a fixed reckoning; } Ar-Rahman-5

{ And made the moon a light in their midst, and made the sun as a (Glorious) Lamp? } Nuh-16

{ It is He who created the night and the day, and the sun and the moon, each gliding in its orbit. } Al-Anbiya'-33

Other examples of Allah's creations are the geographical and chemical isthmus between two seas and between the sea and the river and how the fish in the salty sea are created as palatable as river fish. Indeed each of His creations are unique and contain wisdom.

{ The two seas are not alike. The one is sweet, thirst-quenching, and pleasant to drink from, while the other is salty and bitter. Yet from each you eat fresh fish and extract ornaments to wear, and in each you see the ships ploughing through the waves so that you may seek His bounty and so that you may feel thankful. } Fatir-12

Almighty Allah always warns us not to try to mess with the laws of His creation in the universe to perpetuate life. Did humans obey Their Lord?

{ Corruption has appeared on land and sea because of the evil which the hands of men have done: and so He will make them taste the fruit of some of their doings, so that they may turn back from evil. } Ar-Room-41

Because humans are ignorant and some do not even believe in Allah, they disobeyed Allah and abused the environment created by Allah. We are all now suffering from environmental pollution, weather volatility, and diseases.

....

Other Qur'anic Verses in the Painting:

{ So wait patiently for the Judgement of your Lord -- you are certainly under Our watchful eye. And glorify and celebrate the praises of your Lord when you rise up [from your sleep]. (48) Extol His glory at night, and at the setting of the stars. } At-Tur-48&49

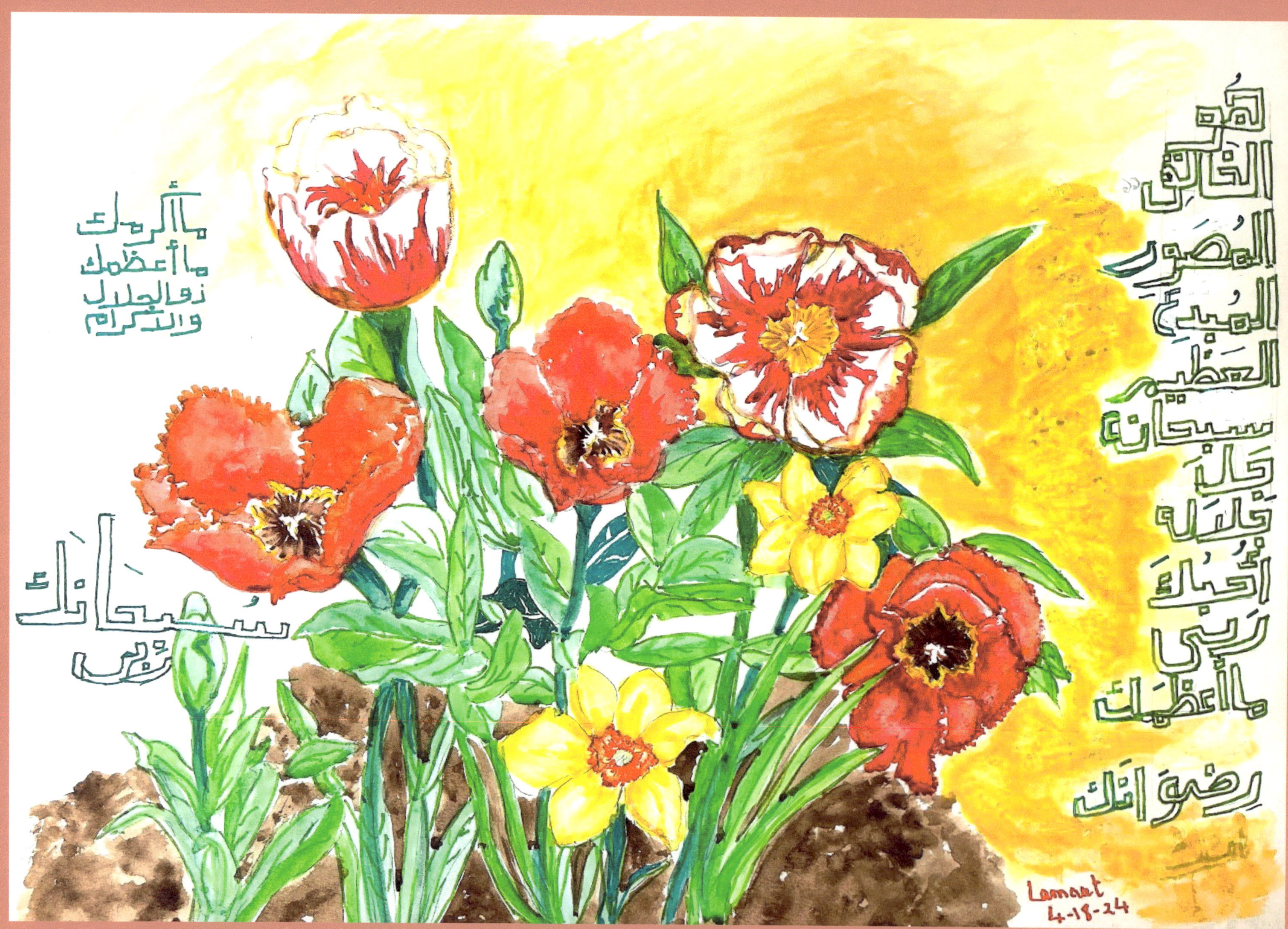
هو الخالق المصور المبدع العظيم سبحانه جلّ جلاله أحبك ربي يا أعظمك با أعظمك رضوانك
ما أكرمك ما أعظمك ذو الجلال والإكرام
سبحانك ربي
Lamaat
4-18-24

Spring Blossoms

I often find peace when reciting the most beautiful descriptive names of Allah Ta'ala. For example:

The Most Gracious - الرحمن, The Most Merciful - الرحيم, The One - الواحد, The Creator - الخالق,

The Almighty - القوي, The Forgiving - الغفور, The Affectionate - الودود and The All Wise - الحكيم.

And I feel close to His Noor and His Grace.

How beautiful are Allah's creation, the spring flowers. When the spring season starts in North America, the flower bulbs wake up after the winter frost, the flower follicles buried in the soil wake up with the permission of Allah - one by one - to please us with the beauty of their buds. It is like a beautiful theatrical show. Each flower type takes its turn. Then the flower fades away and the green leaves take over.

Here are the white and violet Crocus, followed by the orange-yellow Daffodil, then followed by the yellow flower Forsythia, followed by the multi-colored Tulip, then the white and pink flowers of Cherry trees, Magnolias of all kinds and their beautiful fragrance, and then the beautiful Ginkgo trees.

The leaves of the Ginkgo tree have a fan-like appearance that gives the tree a special beauty. As the summer approaches, the lemony scented Freesia emerges, the butterflies flutter through the air, and the Iris and Roses bloom next. The beautiful show continues as a gift and grace from the Creator, Allah, Glory be to Him. All praise to Allah.

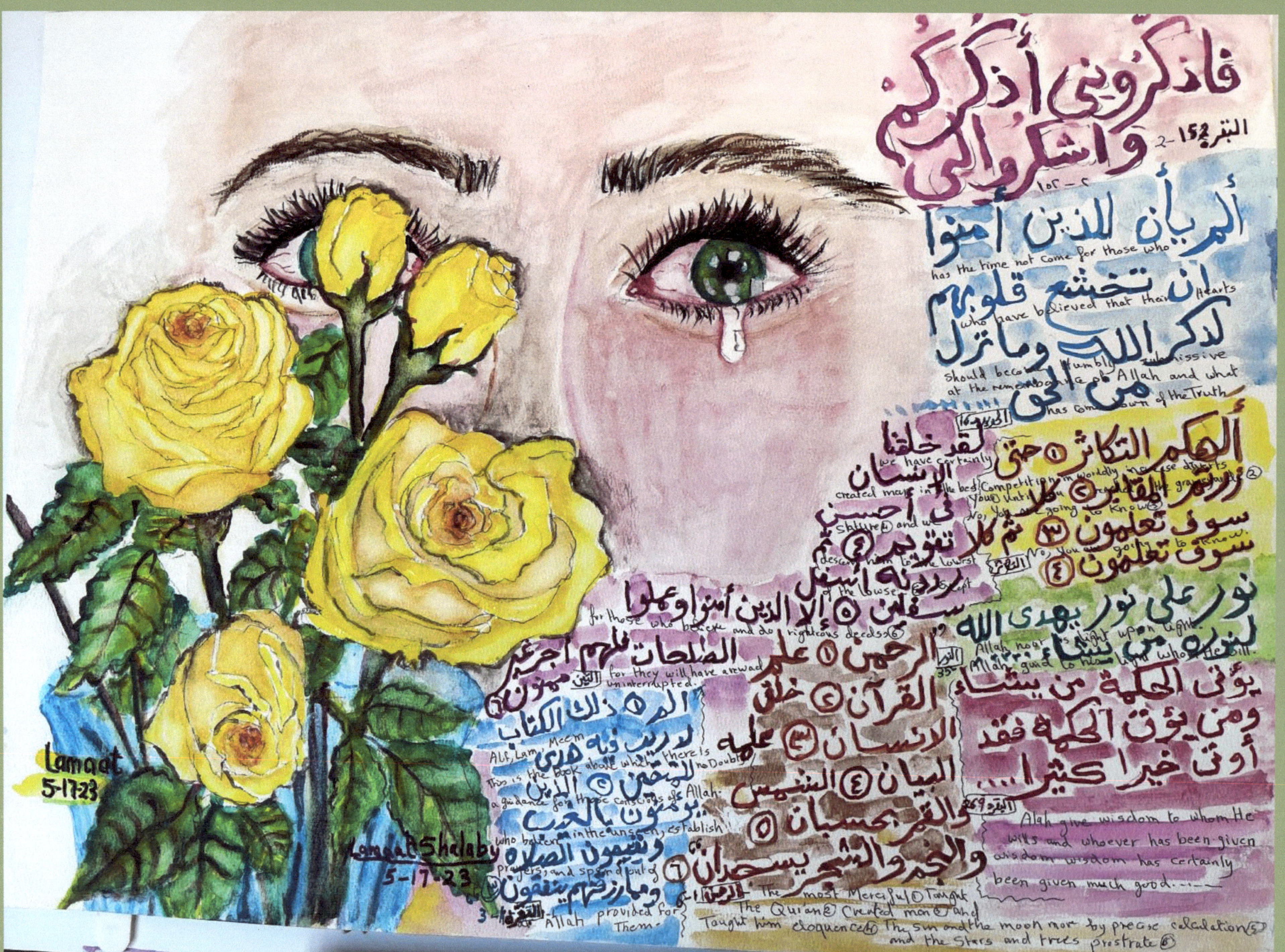

Lamaat
5-17-23
WaaaA Shelaby
5-17-23

A Tear of Humility

This was the second painting in my collection since I started to enrich my watercolor paintings with the Noor of Allah's words.

I felt a sense of guilt – like tears in my heart at mankind's inadequacy to appreciate Allah's creations, wisdom and compassion.

{ Has the time not come for the faithful when their hearts in all humility should engage in the remembrance of God and of the revelation of truth, so that they should not become like those who were given the Book before them, whose hearts with the passage of time became hardened and many of whom were disobedient? } Al-Hadid-16

My only comfort was to remember that Allah is most forgiving for those whose hearts are connected to His Noor.

{ So remember Me; I will remember you. Be thankful to Me and do not be ungrateful. } Al-Baqara-152

I also seek comfort by joining all creatures on Earth in praying to Allah and reciting the Qur'an, Allah's words of Noor.

{ He grants wisdom to whom He wills; and whoever is granted wisdom has indeed been granted abundant wealth. Yet none bear this in mind except those endowed with understanding. } Al-Baqara-269

I still feel this guilt, and I cherish it because it reminds me to preserve my prayers and to follow Allah's guidance in all my actions.

....

Other Qur'anic Verses in the Painting:

{ Alif Lam Mim. (1) This is the Book; there is no doubt in it. It is a guide for those who are mindful of God, (2) who believe in the unseen, and are steadfast in prayer, and spend out of what We have provided them with; (3) } Al-Baqara -1-3

{ God is the light of the heavens and the earth. His light may be compared to a niche containing a lamp, the lamp inside a crystal of star-like brilliance lit from a blessed olive tree, neither of the east nor of the west. The [luminous] oil is as if ready to burn without even touching it. Light upon light; God guides to His light whom He will. God draws such comparisons for mankind; God has full knowledge of everything. } An-Noor-35

{ The Merciful (1) who taught the Qur'an -- (2) He created man (3) and He taught him speech. (4) The sun and the moon move according to a fixed reckoning; (5) the stars and the trees bend in prostration. (6) } Ar-Rahman-1-6

{ We have indeed created man in the best of mold, (4) then We cast him down as the lowest of the low, (5) except for those who believe and do good deeds -- theirs shall be an unending reward! (6) } At-Tin-4-6

{ Greed for more and more distracted you [from God] (1) till you reached the grave. (2) But you will soon come to know. (3) But you will soon come to know. (4) } At-Takathur-1-4

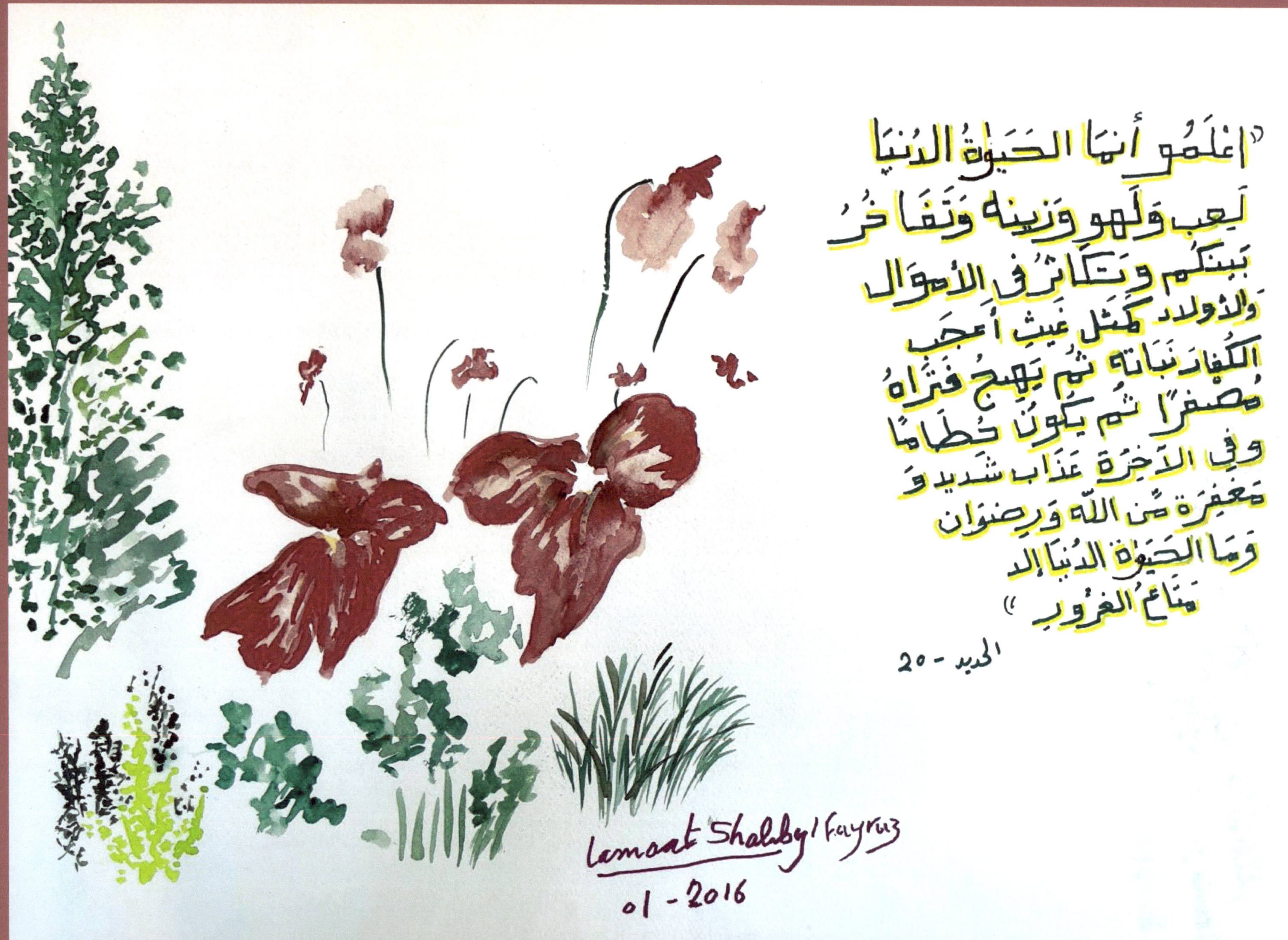

" اعلموا أنما الحياة الدنيا لعب ولهو وزينة وتفاخر بينكم وتكاثر في الأموال والأولاد كمثل غيث أعجب الكفار نباته ثم يهيج فتراه مصفرا ثم يكون حطاما وفي الآخرة عذاب شديد ومغفرة من الله ورضوان وما الحياة الدنيا إلا متاع الغرور "
الحديد - 20
Lamaat Shalaby / Fayruz
01 - 2016

Life to Earn Eternity

This is a painting that I started with my youngest granddaughter, Fayruz, and I like its simplicity. I remembered verse 20 of Surah Al-Hadid and verse 32 of Surah Al-An'am.

{ Never forget that the life of this world is only a game and a passing delight, a show, and mutual boasting and trying to outrival each other in riches and children. It is like the growth of vegetation after the rain, which delights the planter, but which then withers away, turns yellow and becomes worthless stubble. In the life to come there will be a terrible punishment, or God's forgiveness and approval: the life of this world is nothing but means of deception. } Al-Hadid-20

And

{ The life of this world is but a play and a pastime. Surely the Home of the Hereafter is best for those who fear God. Will you not understand? } Al-An'am-32

Glory be to You, Allah. We have been told and warned of the truth of this worldly life. It is a test and a demise and the hereafter is good and lasting. The Almighty has explained the stages of life for us and how they distract us from piety with their temptations and our weakness.

We spend our childhood in play and fun, and in the period of puberty, we focus on our appearance and how to impress others and how to get a top-notch education or job. As time passes by, we spend years focusing on having children and accumulating wealth and property. Then we reach the stage of old age when we will not be able to compensate for the time that has already passed in vain and we didn't prepare enough for the Hereafter!

Glory be to Allah, Almighty, as He has warned us in Surah At-Takathur verses 1 to 8.

{ Greed for more and more distracted you [from God] (1) till you reached the grave. (2) But you will soon come to know. (3) But you will soon come to know. (4) Indeed, were you to know the truth with certainty, (5) you would see the fire of Hell. (6) You would see it with the eye of certainty. (7) Then on that Day you shall be questioned about your worldly favors. (8) } At-Takathur-1-8

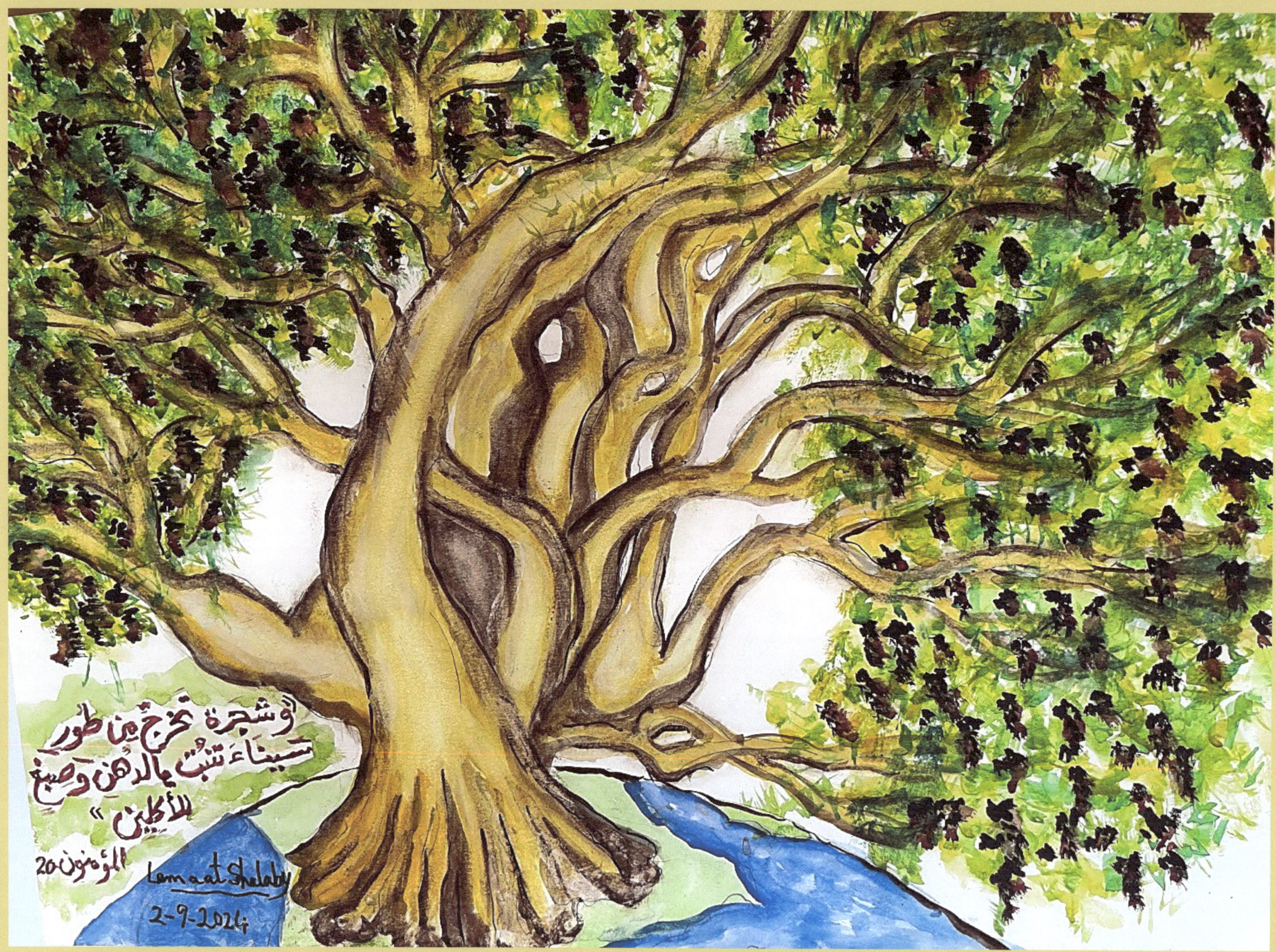

وشجرةٌ تخرج من طور سيناء تنبت بالدُهن وصبغٍ للآكلين «
المؤمنون 20
Lamaat Shelaby
2-9-2024

A Tree growing in Mount Sinai

A verse,

{And a tree growing on Mount Sinai which produces oil and a condiment for those who eat it. } Al-Mu'menoon-20

This has always been explained that it is a reference to the Olive Tree, but what is our conclusive evidence? Allah knows Best. It may also be a sign from Allah (SWT) in reference to another tree in Mount At-Tur in Sinai.

I wish researchers among the believers would search for the types of trees that grow in the wild on Mount At-Tur in Sinai. Are they olive trees or are there other kinds of trees yet to be discovered and have great benefit for us?

I truly enjoy reflecting on the interpretation of Qur'anic verses and reciting them. Oh, Allah forgive me if I make a mistake. I am your servant and I will preserve my covenant to you. Glory be to You.

طه ﴿١﴾ مَا أَنزَلْنَا عَلَيْكَ الْقُرْآنَ لِتَشْقَىٰ ﴿٢﴾ إِلَّا تَذْكِرَةً لِّمَن يَخْشَىٰ ﴿٣﴾

طه ١-٤

يس ﴿١﴾ وَالْقُرْآنِ الْحَكِيمِ ﴿٢﴾ إِنَّكَ لَمِنَ الْمُرْسَلِينَ ﴿٣﴾ عَلَىٰ صِرَاطٍ مُّسْتَقِيمٍ ﴿٤﴾

يس ١-٤

وَالضُّحَىٰ ﴿١﴾ وَاللَّيْلِ إِذَا سَجَىٰ ﴿٢﴾ مَا وَدَّعَكَ رَبُّكَ وَمَا قَلَىٰ ﴿٣﴾

الضحى ١-٣

أَلَمْ نَشْرَحْ لَكَ صَدْرَكَ ﴿١﴾ وَوَضَعْنَا عَنكَ وِزْرَكَ ﴿٢﴾ الَّذِي أَنقَضَ ظَهْرَكَ ﴿٣﴾ وَرَفَعْنَا لَكَ ذِكْرَكَ ﴿٤﴾

الشرح ١-٤

إِنِّي أَنَا رَبُّكَ فَاخْلَعْ نَعْلَيْكَ إِنَّكَ بِالْوَادِ الْمُقَدَّسِ طُوًى ﴿١٢﴾ وَأَنَا اخْتَرْتُكَ فَاسْتَمِعْ لِمَا يُوحَىٰ ﴿١٣﴾ إِنَّنِي أَنَا اللَّهُ لَا إِلَٰهَ إِلَّا أَنَا فَاعْبُدْنِي وَأَقِمِ الصَّلَاةَ لِذِكْرِي ﴿١٤﴾

طه ١٢-١٤

ن وَالْقَلَمِ وَمَا يَسْطُرُونَ ﴿١﴾ مَا أَنتَ بِنِعْمَةِ رَبِّكَ بِمَجْنُونٍ ﴿٢﴾ وَإِنَّ لَكَ لَأَجْرًا غَيْرَ مَمْنُونٍ ﴿٣﴾ وَإِنَّكَ لَعَلَىٰ خُلُقٍ عَظِيمٍ ﴿٤﴾ فَسَتُبْصِرُ وَيُبْصِرُونَ ﴿٥﴾ بِأَييِّكُمُ الْمَفْتُونُ ﴿٦﴾

القلم ١-٦

إِذْ أَوْحَيْنَا إِلَىٰ أُمِّكَ مَا يُوحَىٰ ﴿٣٨﴾ أَنِ اقْذِفِيهِ فِي التَّابُوتِ فَاقْذِفِيهِ فِي الْيَمِّ فَلْيُلْقِهِ الْيَمُّ بِالسَّاحِلِ يَأْخُذْهُ عَدُوٌّ لِّي وَعَدُوٌّ لَّهُ وَأَلْقَيْتُ عَلَيْكَ مَحَبَّةً مِّنِّي وَلِتُصْنَعَ عَلَىٰ عَيْنِي ﴿٣٩﴾

طه ٣٨-٣٩

وَاصْطَنَعْتُكَ لِنَفْسِي ﴿٤١﴾ اذْهَبْ أَنتَ وَأَخُوكَ بِآيَاتِي وَلَا تَنِيَا فِي ذِكْرِي ﴿٤٢﴾ اذْهَبَا إِلَىٰ فِرْعَوْنَ إِنَّهُ طَغَىٰ ﴿٤٣﴾

طه ٤١-٤٤

سُبْحَانَكَ

Lamaat Shalaby
01-2024

The Prophets' Connections

I drew this painting at the beginning of my realization that the Noble Qur'an contains a lot of affectionate communications between Allah, The Almighty and His Prophets.

In this painting, I selected some verses which contain communication between Allah (SWT) and Prophet Muhammad, peace be upon him, and Prophet Musa, peace be upon him.

Allah reassures Prophet Muhammad, peace be upon him, that the goal of assigning him with the message of Islam is not to make him suffer, but rather to remind those who fear and to guide them to the right path.

{ Ta Ha (1) We have not sent the Qur'an down to you to distress you, (2) but only as an exhortation for him who fears God; (3) } Ta-Ha-1-3

{ Ya Seen. (1) By the Qur'an, full of wisdom, (2) you are indeed one of the messengers (3) on a straight path, (4) with a revelation sent down by the Mighty One, the Merciful, (5) } Ya-Seen-1-5

Allah comforted his prophet and assured him that he was not crazy as the non-believers claimed. Allah also promised that He has a great reward for Prophet Muhammad, and that He did not forget him by the interruption of revelation for a short period of time.

{ Nun. By the pen, and all that they write! (1) By the grace of your Lord, you are not a mad man. (2) Most surely, you will have a never-ending reward. (3) For you are truly of a sublime character. (4) Soon you will see, as will they, (5) which of you is a prey to madness. (6) } Al-Qalam-1-6

{ By the glorious morning light; (1) and by the night when it darkens, (2) your Lord has not forsaken you, nor is He displeased with you, (3) }

Adh-Dhuha-1-3

Allah Almighty reminded Prophet Muhammad in Surah Ad-Duha and Ash-Sharh that He has blessed him before with people who cared for him as an orphan and gave him guidance to the religion of truth and promised him that after all these hardships he would be in ease and promised him the highest level in Jannah … Al- Makam Al-Mahmoud.

{ and the Hereafter will indeed be better for you than the present life; (4) soon you will be gratified with what your Lord will give you. (5) Did He not find you orphaned and shelter you? (6) Did He not find you wandering, and give you guidance? (7) Did He not find you in want, and make you free from want? (8) } Adh-Dhuha-4-8

{ Have We not lifted up your heart, (1) and removed your burden (2) that weighed so heavily on your back, and (3) have We not given you high renown? (4) } Ash-Sharh-1-4

To be continued on next pages.

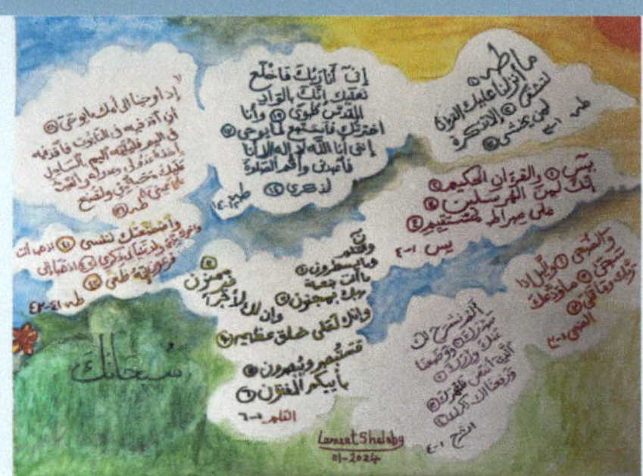

The Prophets' Connections (continued 1)

Listen to the first words of Allah (SWT) to Prophet Musa, peace be upon him:

{ I am your Lord! Take off your shoes, for you are in the sacred valley of Tuwa. (12) I have chosen you. So listen to what is being revealed. (13) I am God. There is no deity save Me; so worship Me alone, and say your prayers in My remembrance. (14) } Ta-Ha-12-14

And when Allah (SWT) reminded him of his childhood story:

{ when We revealed Our will to your mother, saying, (38) "'Put him into a chest, then cast it into the river. The river will cast it on to the bank, and there he shall be taken up by an enemy of Mine and his.' I showered My love on you so that you might be reared under My watchful eye. (39) } Ta-Ha-38&39

{ And I have prepared you for Myself. (41) Go, you and your brother, with My signs, and do not be remiss in remembering Me. (42) Go, both of you to Pharaoh, for he has transgressed all bounds. (43) } Ta-Ha-41-43

And what an honor when Allah Almighty says to Prophet Musa, peace be upon him:

" I have chosen you..." Ta-Ha -13

And, " And I have prepared you for myself.. .." Ta-Ha-41

There are more of these affectionate communications between Allah (SWT) and other Prophets.

For example when Allah Taala tested Prophet Ibrahim, peace be upon him and he passed all tests. Allah said:

{ When his Lord tested Abraham with certain commands and he fulfilled them, He said, "I will make you a leader of people." Abraham asked, "And what of my descendants?" He answered, "My covenant does not extend to the transgressors."} Al-Baqara-124

Another example is what Allah (SWT) said about Prophet Isa, peace be upon him:

{ God said, "O Jesus, I shall take you to Me and will raise you up to Me and shall clear you [of the calumnies] of the disbelievers, and shall place those who follow you above those who deny the truth, until the Day of Judgement; then to Me shall all return and I will judge between you regarding your disputes.} Al-'Imran- 55

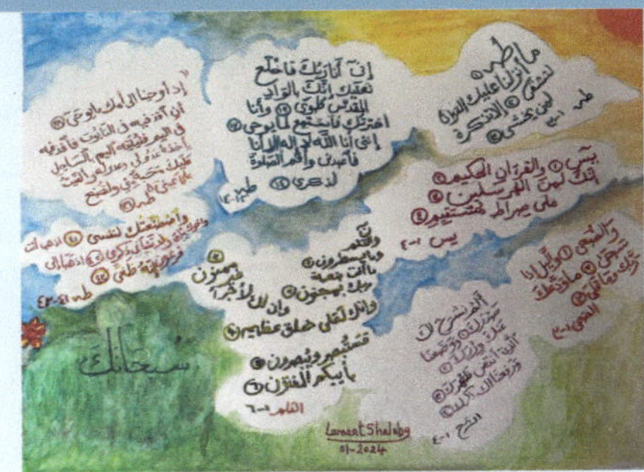

The Prophets' Connections (continued 2)

And,

And what a marvelous interaction between Prophet Nuh, peace be upon him, and Allah (SWT) when the flood drowned the world as punishment for their disbelief. Prophet Nuh called on Allah (SWT) to save his son from drowning. Then he was made aware of the truth from Allah Almighty that his son was not righteous and would be punished because of this.

{ Noah called out to his Lord, saying, "My Lord, my son was a part of my family. Your promise was surely true. You are the most just of all judges." (45) God said, "Noah, he was not one of your family. For, indeed, he was unrighteous in his conduct. Do not question Me about something of which you have no knowledge; I admonish you lest you become like an ignorant man." (46) } Hud-45&46

There is a lot to learn from these interactions. No person carries the sin of another. Every person is responsible for his own choices and actions. It is possible that a righteous person could be afflicted by a sinful child or family member. It is not blood relation that defines righteousness -rather it is our actions and intentions.

I stopped at Surah Ash-Shura, which includes stories of seven Prophets, when I realized that each Prophet told his people the same message.

These verses were mentioned in the story of Hud. { Their brother Hud said to them, "Will you not fear God? (124) I am a trustworthy messenger for you: (125) fear God, then, and obey me. (126) I ask no recompense of you; my reward is only with the Lord of the Universe. (127) } Ash-Shura-124-127

And were repeated by Prophets Nuh, Saleh, Lut and Shuaib, peace be upon them all.

The below verses were also repeated by each Prophet to his people; Musa, Ibrahim, Nuh, Hud, Saleh, Lut and Shuaib, peace be upon them, which are literally identical in words and meaning.

{ Surely in that there is a sign; yet most of them do not believe: (67) truly, your Lord is the Mighty One, the Merciful. (68) } Ash-Shura-67&68

This is an assurance that the message of all prophets and messengers is one and the same – the One Message from Allah Almighty.

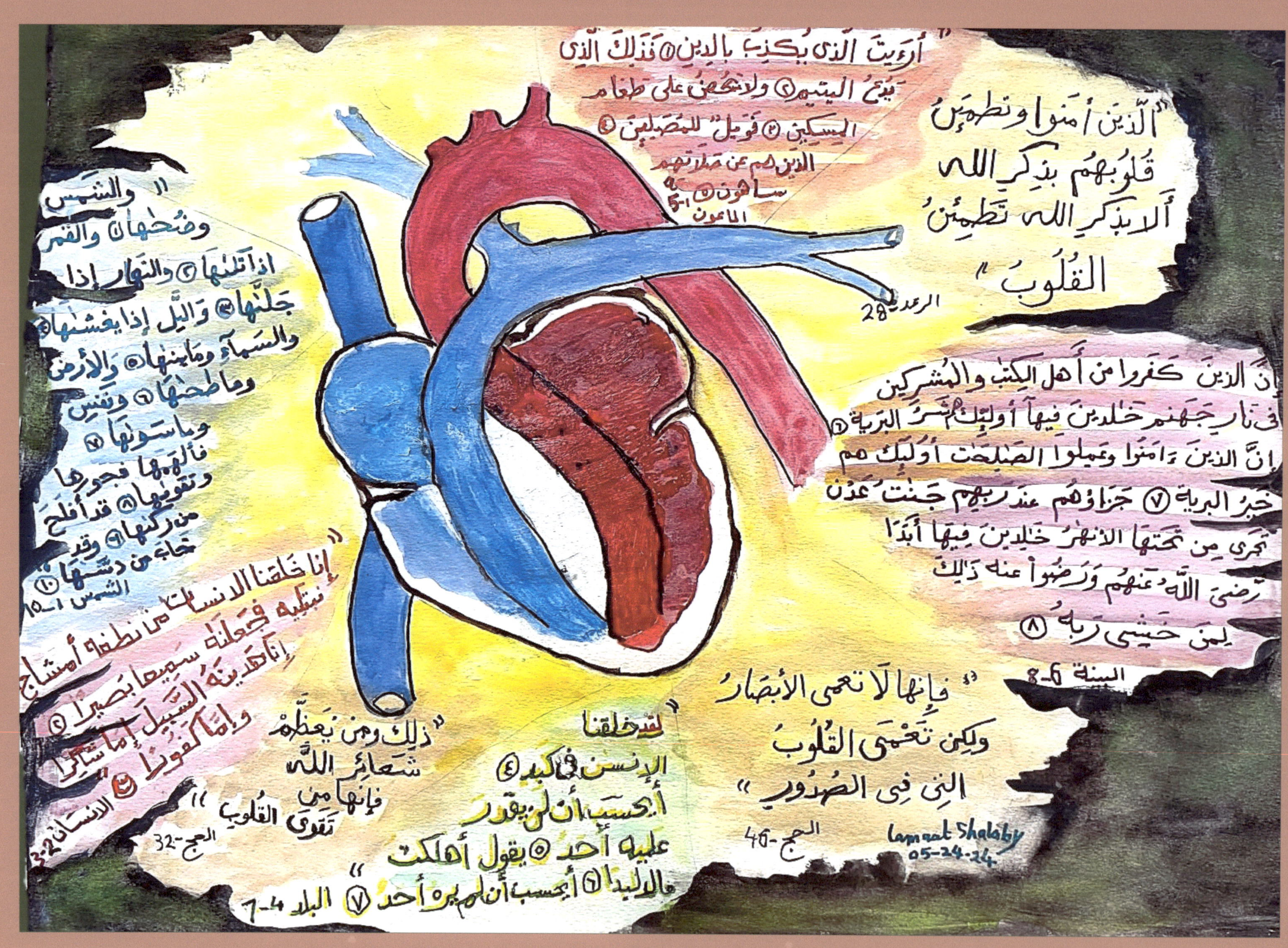

أرأيت الذي يكذب بالدين ۝ فذلك الذي يدع اليتيم ۝ ولا يحض على طعام المسكين ۝ فويل للمصلين ۝ الذين هم عن صلاتهم ساهون ۝ الذين هم يراؤون ۝ ويمنعون الماعون ۝
الذين آمنوا وتطمئن قلوبهم بذكر الله ألا بذكر الله تطمئن القلوب
الرعد 28
إن الذين كفروا من أهل الكتاب والمشركين في نار جهنم خالدين فيها أولئك هم شر البرية ۝ إن الذين آمنوا وعملوا الصالحات أولئك هم خير البرية ۝ جزاؤهم عند ربهم جنات عدن تجري من تحتها الأنهار خالدين فيها أبدا رضي الله عنهم ورضوا عنه ذلك لمن خشي ربه ۝
البينة 6-8
فإنها لا تعمى الأبصار ولكن تعمى القلوب التي في الصدور
الحج 46
Lamaat Shalaby
05-24-24
والشمس وضحاها ۝ والقمر إذا تلاها ۝ والنهار إذا جلاها ۝ والليل إذا يغشاها ۝ والسماء وما بناها ۝ والأرض وما طحاها ۝ ونفس وما سواها ۝ فألهمها فجورها وتقواها ۝ قد أفلح من زكاها ۝ وقد خاب من دساها ۝
الشمس 1-10
إنا خلقنا الإنسان من نطفة أمشاج نبتليه فجعلناه سميعا بصيرا ۝ إنا هديناه السبيل إما شاكرا وإما كفورا ۝
الإنسان 2-3
ذلك ومن يعظم شعائر الله فإنها من تقوى القلوب
الحج 32
لقد خلقنا الإنسان في كبد ۝ أيحسب أن لن يقدر عليه أحد ۝ يقول أهلكت مالا لبدا ۝ أيحسب أن لم يره أحد ۝
البلد 4-7

Thinking Hearts

The heart is one of the great miracles of Allah's creation. This organ is created at the beginning of the development of the fetus in the mother's womb. It beats continuously day and night as long as the fetus or the human being is alive. Mankind has no control over his body's organs. Allah Almighty created them and made them work involuntarily.

The heart is mentioned repeatedly in the Qur'an but the word brain is not mentioned. Maybe because the heart plays the main role in perception and decision making. Perhaps the mind's function is to gather information and present it to the heart to make the decision. Modern science is discovering that the heart has a special neural connection to the brain and that the impulses from the heart to the brain are more than those from the brain to the heart.   **Ref. 2**

Verse 46 of Surah Al-Hajj refers to the heart as the part of the human that accepts or denies facts.

{ Have these people not traveled through the land to make their hearts understand and let their ears hear; the truth is that it is not the eyes that are blind but the hearts that are in the chests that are blinded.} Al-Hajj-46

And Allah Almighty described in the Qur'an that the bad deeds of the sinful aggressor had blinded his heart.

{ Those who deny the Day of Judgement. (11) No one denies it except for the evil aggressor. (12) When Our revelations are conveyed to him, he says, "Fables of the ancients!" (13) No! Their own deeds have cast a veil over their hearts. (14) } Al-Mutaffifin-11-14

Allah Almighty told us that remembering Him reassures our hearts. My interpretation is that the heart is the center of our spiritual pleasure.

{ Those who believe and whose hearts find comfort in the remembrance of God -- surely in the remembrance of God hearts can find comfort. } Ar-Ra'd -28

And Allah Knows Best.

…………………………………………….

Other Qur'anic Verses in the Painting:

{ We created man from a drop of mingled fluid so that We might try him; We gave him hearing and sight; (2) We showed him the way, whether he be grateful or ungrateful.(3) } Al-Insan-2&3

{ Have you seen one who denies the Day of Judgement? (1) Who turns away the orphan, (2) and who does not urge the feeding of the poor? (3) So woe to those who pray (4) but whose hearts are not in their prayer. (5) } Al-Ma'un-1-5

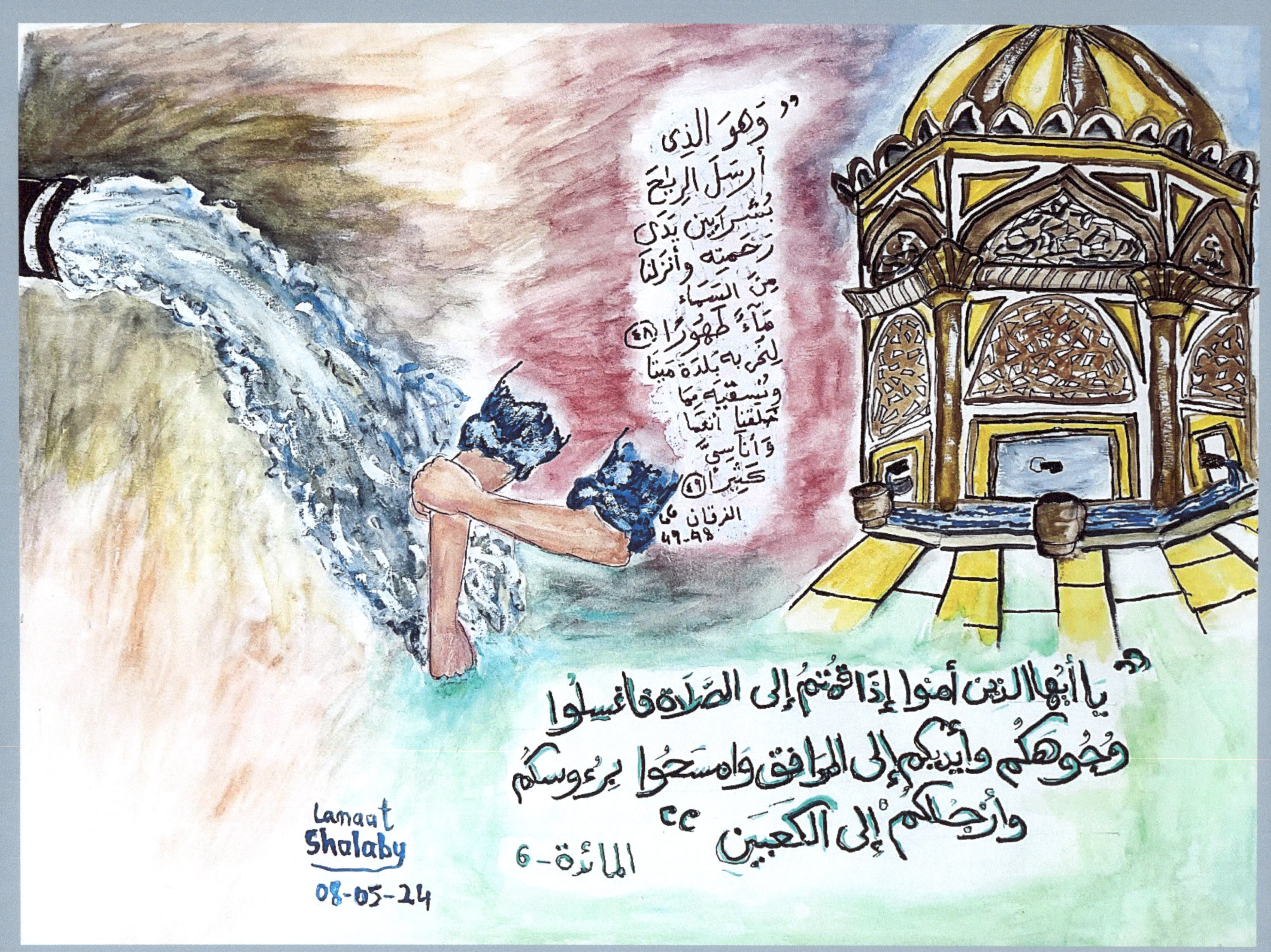

" وَهُوَ الَّذِى أَرْسَلَ الرِّيَاحَ بُشْرًا بَيْنَ يَدَىْ رَحْمَتِهِ وَأَنزَلْنَا مِنَ السَّمَاءِ مَاءً طَهُورًا ۝ لِنُحْيِىَ بِهِ بَلْدَةً مَّيْتًا وَنُسْقِيَهُ مِمَّا خَلَقْنَا أَنْعَامًا وَأَنَاسِىَّ كَثِيرًا ۝
الفرقان من
٤٨-٤٩
" يَا أَيُّهَا الَّذِينَ آمَنُوا إِذَا قُمْتُمْ إِلَى الصَّلَاةِ فَاغْسِلُوا وُجُوهَكُمْ وَأَيْدِيَكُمْ إِلَى الْمَرَافِقِ وَامْسَحُوا بِرُءُوسِكُمْ وَأَرْجُلَكُمْ إِلَى الْكَعْبَيْنِ "
المائدة ٦
Lamaut
Shalaby
08-05-24

Purification of the Body and Soul

I went to perform wudu (ablution) in preparation for salah (prayer) and stopped for a moment to praise Allah, for His wisdom in demanding wudu before salah. Wudu makes a person feel pure and refreshed in preparation for his salah to Allah.

Wudu includes washing the face and arms to the elbow, followed by wiping the head and washing the feet thoroughly.

{ O you who have believed, when you rise to pray, wash your faces and your arms up to the elbows and wipe your heads and [wash] your feet up to the ankles…. } Al-Ma'eda - 6

According to Prophet Muhammad's (PBUH) Sunnah, wudu includes washing the mouth and nose three times. Doesn't this guarantee their cleanliness and hydration without the use of medicines and chemicals. If we do wudu five times a day, this will keep our bodies clean and free from contaminants and instead fills our bodies with energy and joy. This is the perfect purification routine. It is necessary here to mention the mercy of Allah, as He gave us the option of patting a dry and clean surface and wiping our face and hands in the situations where we can't find water for wudu or if we cannot use water for other reasons.

After wudu we face the Qibla (towards the Kaaba in Makkah) for salah. The repeated steps of salah from standing to kneeling to prostrating and reciting the Qur'an are the best exercise for the body and the soul. Allah Almighty has commanded us to perform salah, but He also made it easy for us. If we can't stand to perform salah, then we can perform salah while sitting or even laying down.

In this era, everyone runs treadmills or other gym equipment to have a perfect body. I often wonder to myself though, aren't humans made of both a body and a soul? How do they focus all their time and effort to take care of their bodies only and neglect their souls! Most souls are lost and are thirsty for enlightenment from Allah but no one addresses the soul's needs. Most people follow the crowd, and the crowd follows the misleading media. People waste most of their spare time in idle entertainment to escape addressing the emptiness in their souls. Or worse, they resort to drinking alcohol, therapists, drugs and addiction to try to deal with this emptiness.

Allah Taala created us and the entire universe. He is the only One who knows what is best for us. I pray that I can adhere to Allah's guidance and not to be a follower of the lost souls. I thank Allah and I seek His forgiveness.

....

Other Qur'anic Verses in the Painting:

{ It is He who sends the winds as heralds of His mercy and We send down pure water from the sky, (48) so that We may bring life to a dead land; and slake the thirst of Our creation; cattle and men, in great numbers. (49) } Al-Furqan-48 & 49

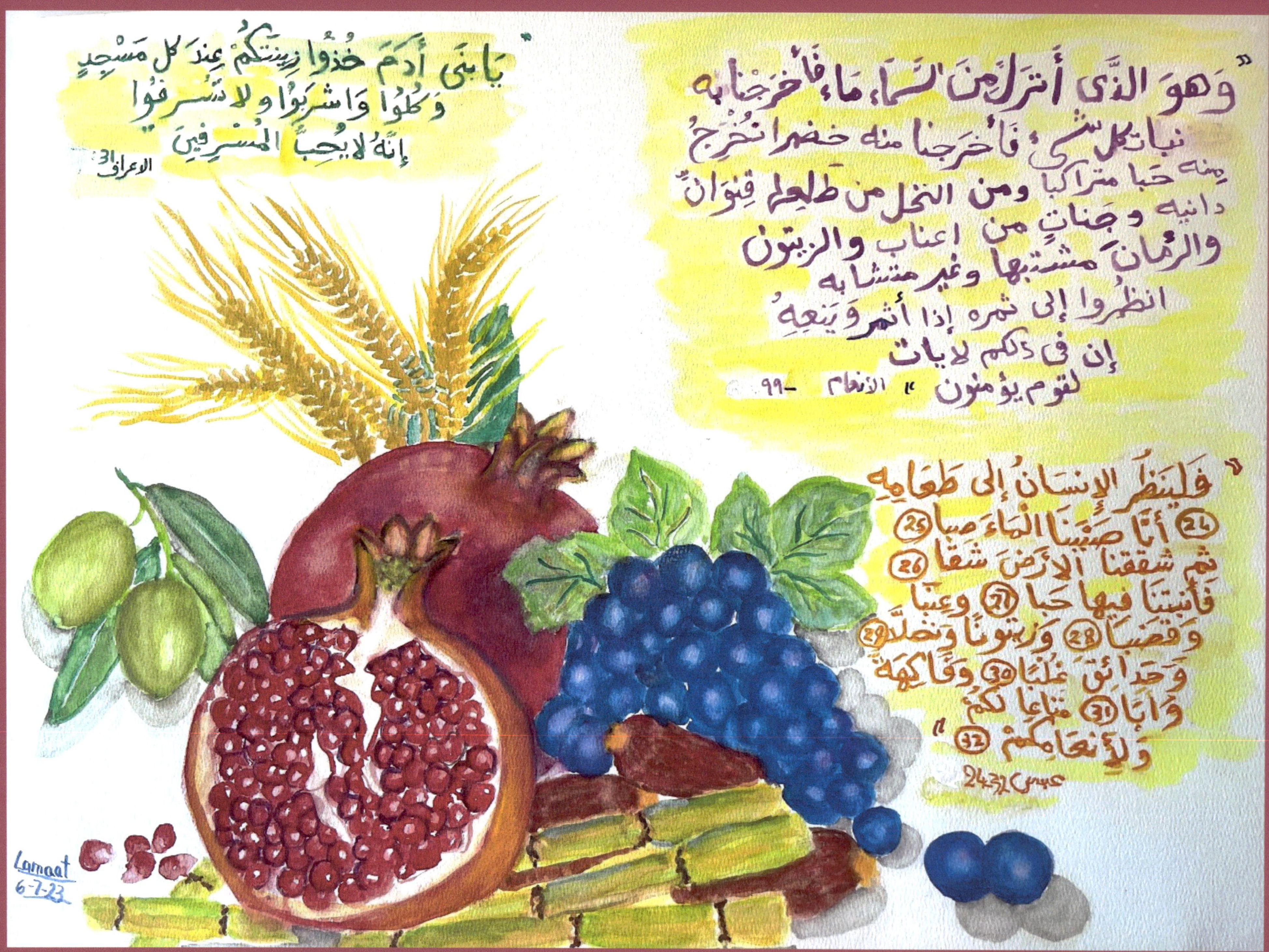

"وَهُوَ الَّذِي أَنزَلَ مِنَ السَّمَاءِ مَاءً فَأَخْرَجْنَا بِهِ نَبَاتَ كُلِّ شَيْءٍ فَأَخْرَجْنَا مِنْهُ خَضِرًا نُّخْرِجُ مِنْهُ حَبًّا مُّتَرَاكِبًا وَمِنَ النَّخْلِ مِن طَلْعِهَا قِنْوَانٌ دَانِيَةٌ وَجَنَّاتٍ مِّنْ أَعْنَابٍ وَالزَّيْتُونَ وَالرُّمَّانَ مُشْتَبِهًا وَغَيْرَ مُتَشَابِهٍ انظُرُوا إِلَى ثَمَرِهِ إِذَا أَثْمَرَ وَيَنْعِهِ إِنَّ فِي ذَلِكُمْ لَآيَاتٍ لِّقَوْمٍ يُؤْمِنُونَ" الأنعام ٩٩
"يَا بَنِي آدَمَ خُذُوا زِينَتَكُمْ عِندَ كُلِّ مَسْجِدٍ وَكُلُوا وَاشْرَبُوا وَلَا تُسْرِفُوا إِنَّهُ لَا يُحِبُّ الْمُسْرِفِينَ" الأعراف ٣١
"فَلْيَنظُرِ الْإِنسَانُ إِلَى طَعَامِهِ ٢٤ أَنَّا صَبَبْنَا الْمَاءَ صَبًّا ٢٥ ثُمَّ شَقَقْنَا الْأَرْضَ شَقًّا ٢٦ فَأَنبَتْنَا فِيهَا حَبًّا ٢٧ وَعِنَبًا وَقَضْبًا ٢٨ وَزَيْتُونًا وَنَخْلًا ٢٩ وَحَدَائِقَ غُلْبًا ٣٠ وَفَاكِهَةً وَأَبًّا ٣١ مَّتَاعًا لَّكُمْ وَلِأَنْعَامِكُمْ ٣٢" عبس ٢٤-٣٢
Lamaat
6-7-23

The Gift of Food and Water

I was preparing a pomegranate fruit for my family. I was fascinated with the shape of the seeds which are full of refreshing crimson red juice and are neatly arranged inside the shiny, white crust. They looked like rubies, stacked in a box of ivory-colored satin. I praised Allah for His Grace and the beauty of His creations. I remembered Surah Al-An'am verse 99:

{ It is He who sends down water from the sky. With it We produce vegetation of all kinds; out of green foliage, We produce clustered grain; and from the date-palm, out of its sheath, We produce bunches of dates hanging low. We produce vineyards and olive groves and pomegranates, alike yet different. Look at their fruit as He causes it to grow and ripen. In this are signs for people who believe. } Al-Anaam-99

I also remembered Surah 'Abasa verses 24-32, Surah Al-Hajj verse 5, and Surah Fussilat verse 39, in which Allah Almighty explains to us how He created the process of germination from water and soil. When the rain falls on the soil, it is absorbed by the seed which swells and cracks to sprout all types of plants: the grass-type like grains and alfalfa, palm-type like dates and coconuts, climber-type such as grapes, and tree-type both single-seed like olives and multi-seed like pomegranates.

{ Let man reflect on the food he eats. (24) We let the rain pour down in torrents (25) and then We cleaved the earth asunder. (26) We make the grain grow out of it, (27) and grape vines and vegetables, (28) and olive trees and date palms (29) and burgeoning enclosed gardens (30) and fruits and fodder (31) as provision for you and for your cattle to enjoy. (32) } 'Abasa-24-32

{ ... You see the earth, dead and barren, but no sooner do We send down rain upon it than it begins to stir and swell, and produce every kind of luxuriant vegetation: } Al-Hajj-5

{ Among His signs is this: you see the earth dry and barren, but when We send down on it water, it stirs and swells: most surely He who gives it life is the giver of life to the dead; surely He has power over all things. } Fussilat-39

He is Allah, the One and Only, Who created everything and we deeply appreciate it. I praise Allah (SWT) and His kindness and wisdom.

{ O Children of Adam, dress yourself properly whenever you are at worship: and eat and drink but do not be wasteful: God does not like wasteful people. } Al-A'raf-31

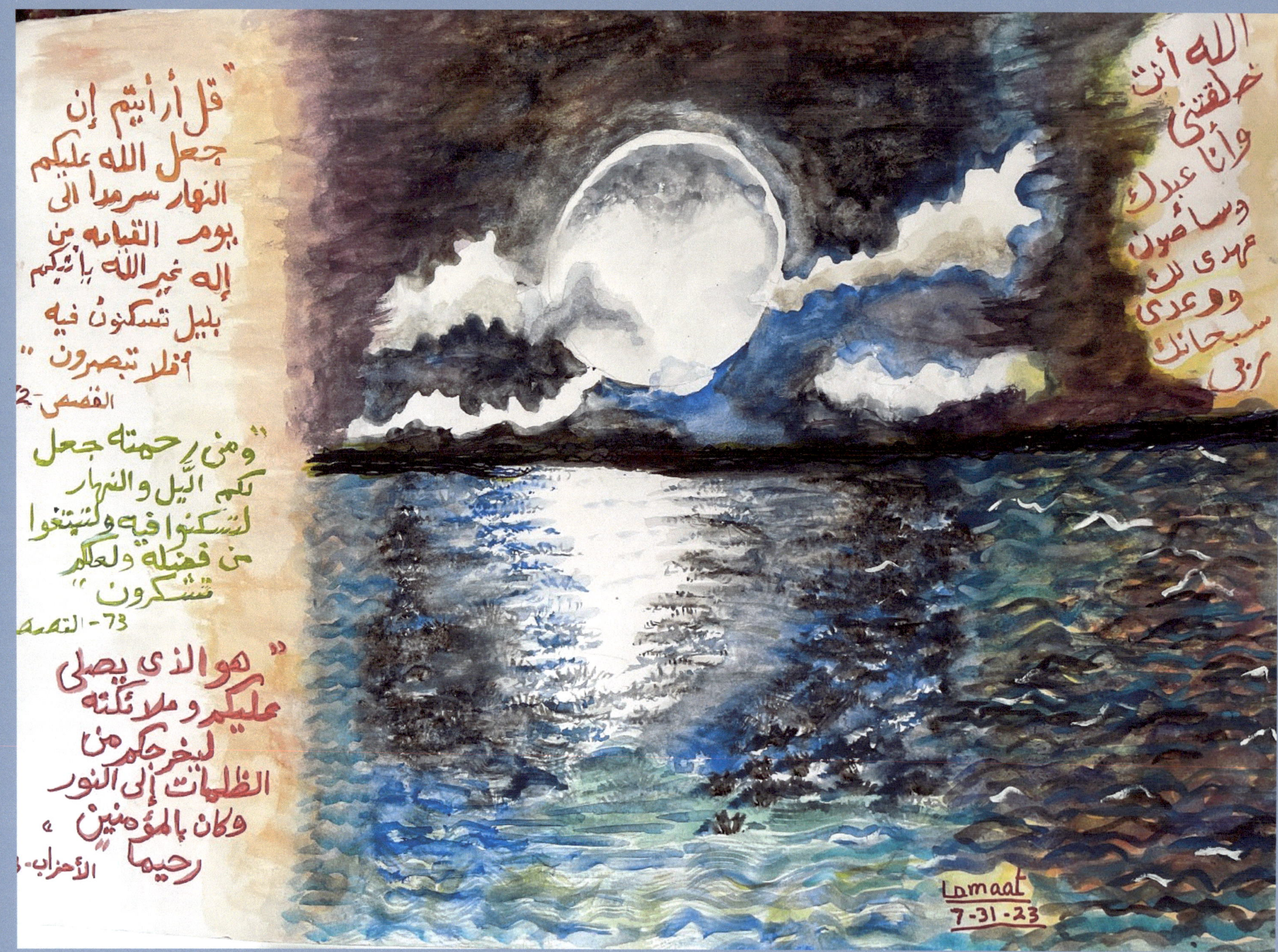
" قل أرأيتم إن جعل الله عليكم النهار سرمدا الى يوم القيامة من إله غير الله يأتيكم بليل تسكنون فيه أفلا تبصرون "
القصص - ٧٢
" ومن رحمته جعل لكم الليل والنهار لتسكنوا فيه ولتبتغوا من فضله ولعلكم تشكرون "
٧٣ - القصص
" هو الذي يصلي عليكم وملائكته ليخرجكم من الظلمات إلى النور وكان بالمؤمنين رحيما "
الأحزاب
الله أنت خلقتني وأنا عبدك وسأصون عهدى لك ووعدى سبحانك ربى
Lamaat
7-31-23

Day and Night

It is a blessing among the great blessings of Allah that He created the cycle of day and night. It is not a permanent night, so plants, food, animals and humans do not perish. And not a permanent day, so the proportion of oxygen and carbon dioxide in the air remains balanced and the living will not die from lack of sleep and exhaustion. But Allah, with His mercy and wisdom, manages the matter and preserves the balance, so that humans and all the living creatures on Earth can live and thrive.

{ Ask them, "Tell me, if God were to extend perpetual night over you till the Day of Judgement, is there any deity other than God that could bring you light? Will you not listen?" (71) Say, "Tell me, if God were to extend perpetual day over you till the Day of Judgement -- is there any deity other than God that could bring you night, in which to rest? Will you not then see?" (72) In His mercy He has made for you the night and the day, during which you may rest, and seek His bounty and be grateful. (73) } Al-Qasas-71-73

I feel as if our souls are drawn to the light of Allah Almighty through our salah. Otherwise our souls – overwhelmed by the nature of our weakness and the continuous temptation of Shaytan - would fall into darkness.

In Surah Al-Ahzab, verse 43, Allah Almighty told us that He sends blessings to us in order to bring us out of the darkness of disbelief and sins to the light of faith and repentance.

{ It is He who sends blessings to you, as do His angels, so that He may bring you out of the darkness into the light. He is most merciful to the believers (43) } Al-Ahzab-43

I remember a conversation between my father and me years ago. He said:

The truth, my daughter, is that each of us has our own spiritual channel of Noor (Enlightenment) from Allah Ta'ala. No one can share it with anyone. If a person chooses to open his heart, he will receive Allah's Noor and Guidance. If his heart is left closed, he will not receive the Noor from Allah and the nourishment of his soul and will remain in the darkness.

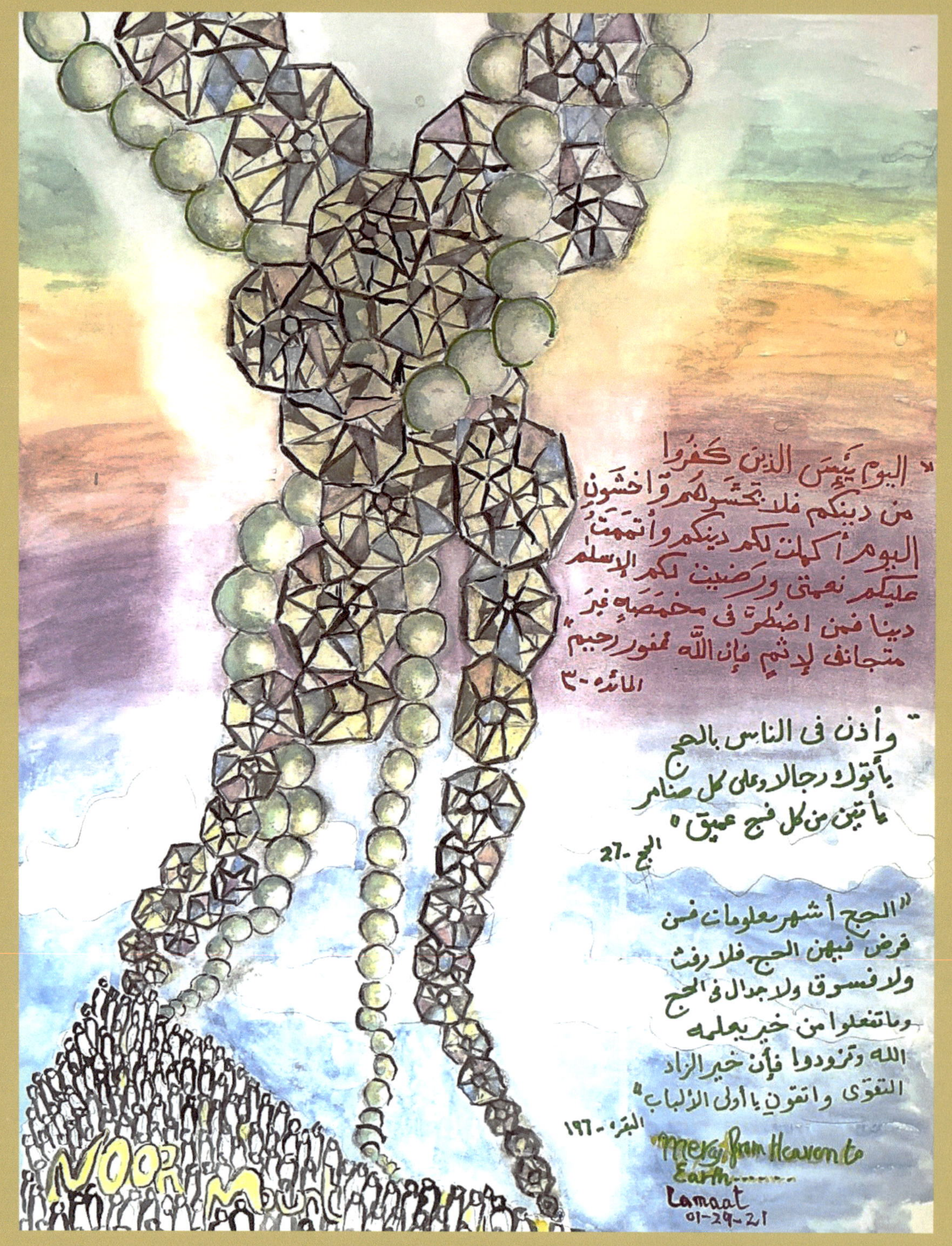
الیوم یئس الذین کفروا
من دینکم فلا تخشوهم واخشون
الیوم اکملت لکم دینکم واتممت
علیکم نعمتی ورضیت لکم الاسلام
دینا فمن اضطر فی مخمصۃ غیر
متجانف لاثم فان الله غفور رحیم
المائدۃ ـ ۳

واذن فی الناس بالحج
یاتوک رجالا وعلی کل ضامر
یاتین من کل فج عمیق
الحج ـ ۲۷

الحج اشهر معلومات فمن
فرض فیهن الحج فلا رفث
ولا فسوق ولا جدال فی الحج
وما تفعلوا من خیر یعلمه
الله وتزودوا فان خیر الزاد
التقوی واتقون یا اولی الالباب
البقرۃ ـ ۱۹۶

Mercy from Heaven to
Earth......
Lamaat
01-29-21

NOOR M

"Today, I have Completed your Religion"

This painting is of a beautiful dream I had on the night of Arafa during my Hajj in 1996.

I saw a sea of pilgrims, dressed in white, praying on Mount Noor. Then a braided rope made of diamonds and pearls, as wide as the horizon, descended from Heaven. The braided rope unraveled and enveloped the pilgrims and all of Mount Noor.

I felt surrounded by blessings - as if Allah's Mercy and Forgiveness was granted at that moment to all the pilgrims. Allah, glory be to Him, is the Most Merciful and the Most Compassionate.

The gathering on the days of Hajj reminds me of Methaq Al Zarr (the covenant taken from all the children of Adam about Monotheism).

Allah Almighty says - in reference to this covenant : { When your Lord brought forth offspring from the loins of the Children of Adam and made them bear witness about themselves, He said, "Am I not your Lord?" They replied, "We bear witness that You are." This He did, lest you should say on the Day of Resurrection, "We had no knowledge of that." } Al-A'raf-172

I will always appreciate Allah's Mercy and miraculous creations.

....

Qur'anic Verses in the Painting:

{ Call mankind to the Pilgrimage. They will come to you, on foot, and on every kind of lean camel, by every distant track } Al-Hajj-27

{ The pilgrimage is in the appointed months. Whoever intends to perform it during them must abstain from indecent speech, from all wicked conduct, and from quarreling while on the pilgrimage. Whatever good you may do, God is aware of it. Make provision for yourselves -- but surely, the best of all provision is God-consciousness. Always be mindful of Me, you that are endowed with understanding. } Al-Baqara-197

{... Today the disbelievers have given up all hope of undermining your faith. So do not fear them; fear Me! Today I have completed your religion for you and completed My blessing upon you, and chosen Islam as your way... } Al-Ma'eda-3

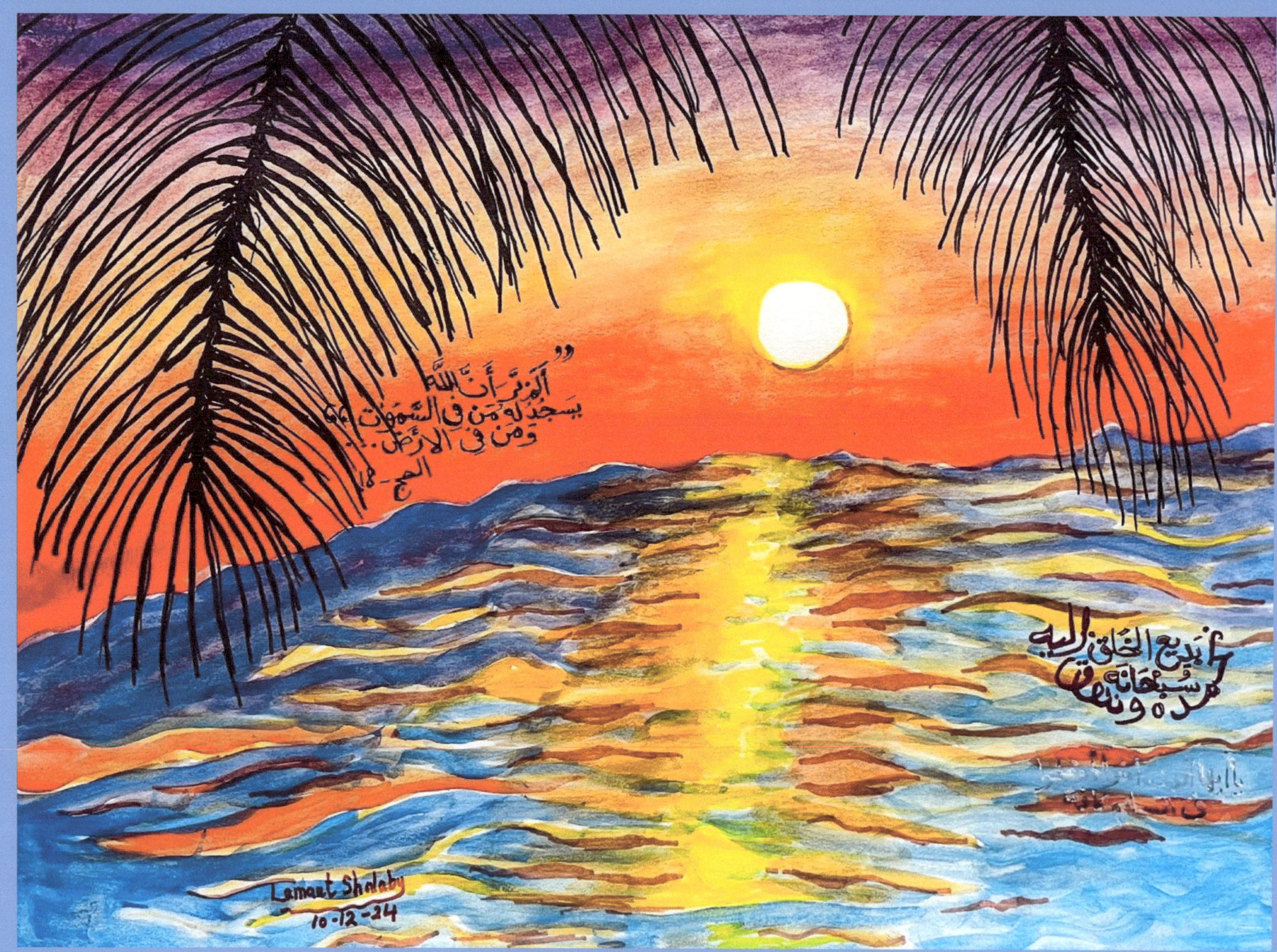

" أَلَمْ تَرَ أَنَّ اللَّهَ يَسْجُدُ لَهُ مَن فِي السَّمَاوَاتِ وَمَن فِي الْأَرْضِ "
الحج
Lamaet Shalaby
10-12-24

38

Nature's Positive Energy

I often think about why we feel peaceful and comfortable when we indulge in nature and natural activities, such as parks, mountains, beaches or watching birds and flowers and playing with young children. The secret may be in this verse:

{ Do you not see that to Allah bow down in submission all those in the heavens and all those on the earth, as well as the sun, the moon, the stars, the mountains, the trees, and all living beings, as well as many humans, while many are deserving of punishment. And whoever Allah disgraces, none can honor. Surely Allah does what He wills. } Al-Hajj-18

Obedience and sujood (prostration) to Allah Ta'ala generates Noor and positive energy around nature. This is what we feel when we immerse ourselves in nature.

One of the most common human diseases nowadays is psychological depression. The most important symptoms are that a person loses the desire for any activity and feels sad and frustrated. Perhaps one of the reasons for this disease is that while seeking comfort man has surrounded himself with many of his industrial inventions such as air-conditioned homes, electrical appliances, manufactured building materials, hours in front of the television and social media, and anxiety and hard work to finance this comfort. He neglected his prayers and the chance to get in touch with His Creator, Allah (SWT).

Humans distanced themselves from the beauty and tranquility of nature and positive energy in the company of trees, birds, beaches, pure air, the sun and the moon. All this robbed has humans of positive energy, and the psychological and organic diseases took over.

Allah Almighty told us that the remedy is in His Remembrance. The soul will derive positive energy from His remembrance; hearts will be reassured. Allah Almighty guided us to help each other, to get to know each other. This removes a sense of loneliness and restores confidence in ourselves. Allah Almighty created for us the warm sun, pure air breeze, birds singing, the beauty of flowers, the water and sea waves - all to refresh the soul and the body.

{ Those who believe and whose hearts find comfort in the remembrance of Allah. Surely in the remembrance of Allah do hearts find comfort.}
Ar-Ra'd-28

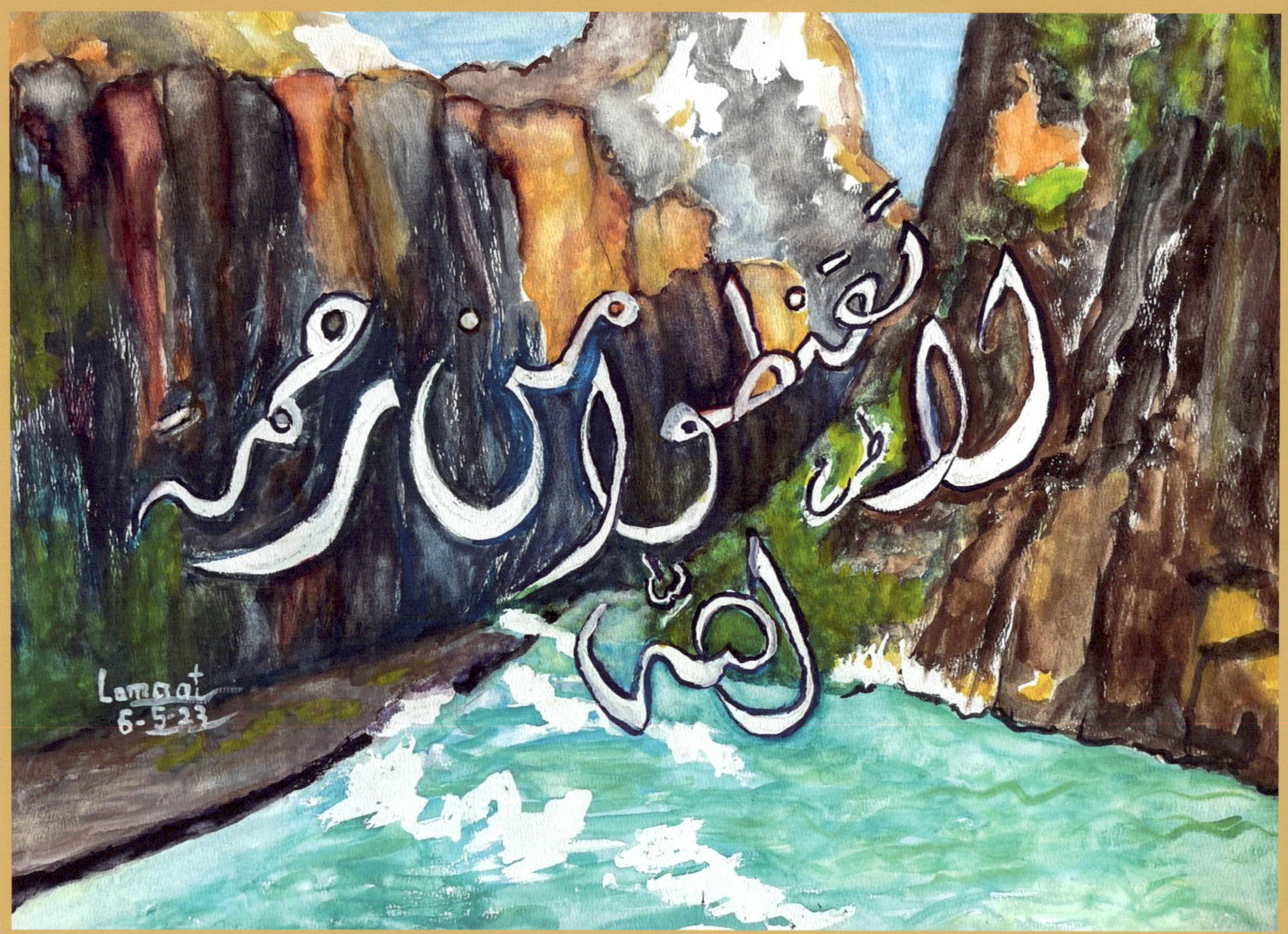

لا تعظموا من رحمه
أسا
Lamaai
6-5-23

Allah's Mercy Has No Limits

When I saw these tall mountains, I remembered several facts that Allah Almighty told us about mountains in the Qur'an. Allah created the mountains to maintain the stability of the earth.

Mountains exist in a wide range of colors. Some are white; others are red or black or in between. Perhaps this is a signal to humans that this variation in color indicates components and materials of precious value to man, such as gold and other minerals. Humans over time have discovered this, and in some instances exploited it for their benefit.

When I looked at the picture of the tall mountains, I thought of how hard it must be to penetrate them. Then, I noticed that there is a passage between them with water running through it. I remembered what Allah told us – to not despair for Allah's mercy encompasses everything. Praise be to Allah.

The Qur'an is a collection of the words of Allah, the Most Powerful. If the Qur'an were revealed to a mountain, it would crumble out of fear of Allah. Here we remember the level of spiritual strength of Prophet Muhammad (PBUH) upon whom the Qur'an was revealed. He carried what the mountain couldn't bear. Let's pray for him to get the highest level in Jannah and do our best to fulfill and follow his message.

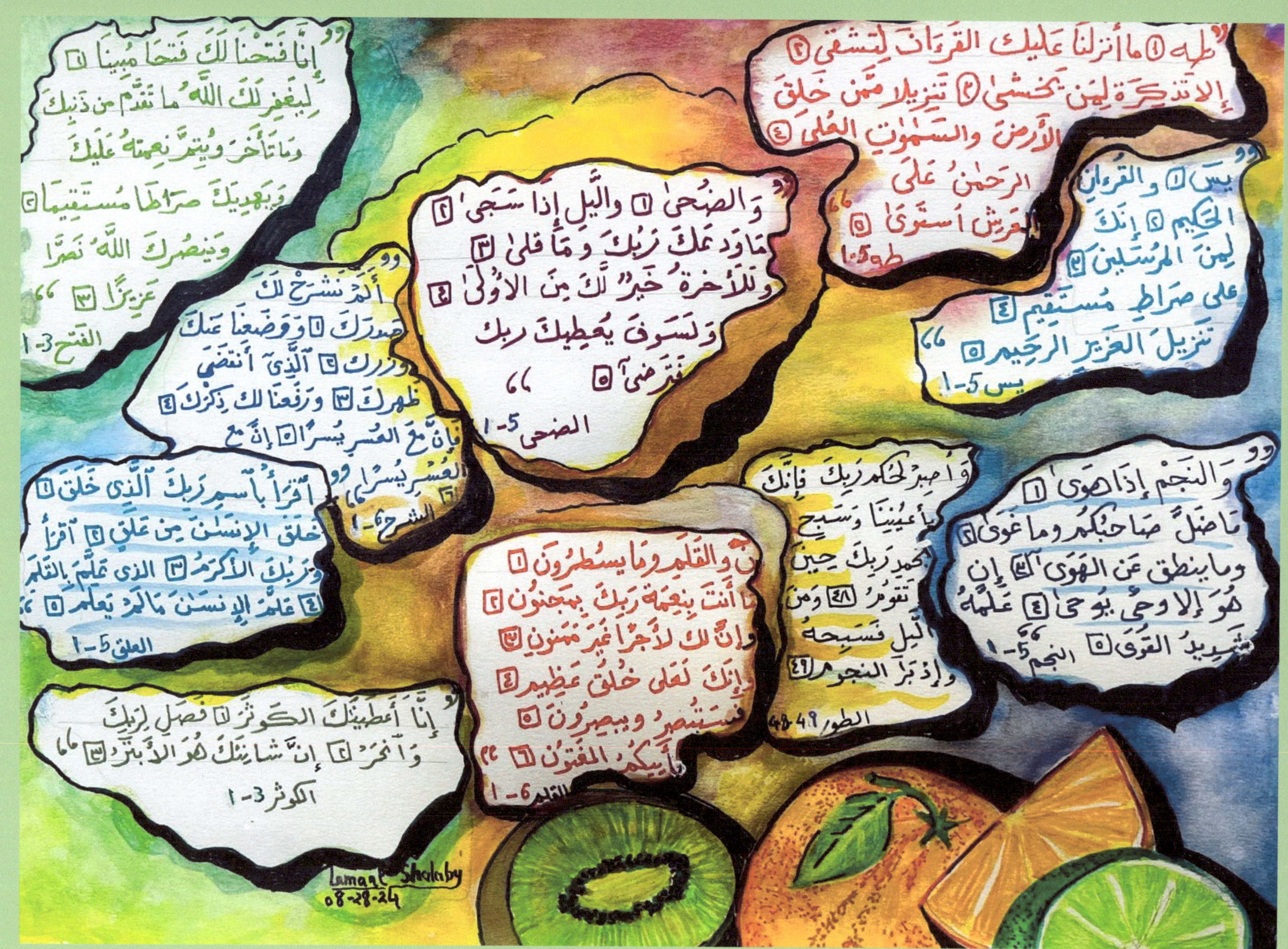

إِنَّا فَتَحْنَا لَكَ فَتْحًا مُّبِينًا ١ لِّيَغْفِرَ لَكَ اللَّهُ مَا تَقَدَّمَ مِن ذَنبِكَ وَمَا تَأَخَّرَ وَيُتِمَّ نِعْمَتَهُ عَلَيْكَ وَيَهْدِيَكَ صِرَاطًا مُّسْتَقِيمًا ٢ وَيَنصُرَكَ اللَّهُ نَصْرًا عَزِيزًا ٣
الفتح ٣-١

أَلَمْ نَشْرَحْ لَكَ صَدْرَكَ ١ وَوَضَعْنَا عَنكَ وِزْرَكَ ٢ الَّذِي أَنقَضَ ظَهْرَكَ ٣ وَرَفَعْنَا لَكَ ذِكْرَكَ ٤ فَإِنَّ مَعَ الْعُسْرِ يُسْرًا ٥ إِنَّ مَعَ الْعُسْرِ يُسْرًا ٦
الشرح ٦-١

اقْرَأْ بِاسْمِ رَبِّكَ الَّذِي خَلَقَ ١ خَلَقَ الْإِنسَانَ مِنْ عَلَقٍ ٢ اقْرَأْ وَرَبُّكَ الْأَكْرَمُ ٣ الَّذِي عَلَّمَ بِالْقَلَمِ ٤ عَلَّمَ الْإِنسَانَ مَا لَمْ يَعْلَمْ ٥
العلق ٥-١

إِنَّا أَعْطَيْنَاكَ الْكَوْثَرَ ١ فَصَلِّ لِرَبِّكَ وَانْحَرْ ٢ إِنَّ شَانِئَكَ هُوَ الْأَبْتَرُ ٣
الكوثر ٣-١

وَالضُّحَى ١ وَاللَّيْلِ إِذَا سَجَى ٢ مَا وَدَّعَكَ رَبُّكَ وَمَا قَلَى ٣ وَلَلْآخِرَةُ خَيْرٌ لَّكَ مِنَ الْأُولَى ٤ وَلَسَوْفَ يُعْطِيكَ رَبُّكَ فَتَرْضَى ٥
الضحى ٥-١

ن وَالْقَلَمِ وَمَا يَسْطُرُونَ ١ مَا أَنتَ بِنِعْمَةِ رَبِّكَ بِمَجْنُونٍ ٢ وَإِنَّ لَكَ لَأَجْرًا غَيْرَ مَمْنُونٍ ٣ وَإِنَّكَ لَعَلَى خُلُقٍ عَظِيمٍ ٤ فَسَتُبْصِرُ وَيُبْصِرُونَ ٥ بِأَييِّكُمُ الْمَفْتُونُ ٦
القلم ٦-١

وَاصْبِرْ لِحُكْمِ رَبِّكَ فَإِنَّكَ بِأَعْيُنِنَا وَسَبِّحْ بِحَمْدِ رَبِّكَ حِينَ تَقُومُ ٤٨ وَمِنَ اللَّيْلِ فَسَبِّحْهُ وَإِدْبَارَ النُّجُومِ ٤٩
الطور ٤٩-٤٨

طه ١ مَا أَنزَلْنَا عَلَيْكَ الْقُرْآنَ لِتَشْقَى ٢ إِلَّا تَذْكِرَةً لِّمَن يَخْشَى ٣ تَنزِيلًا مِّمَّنْ خَلَقَ الْأَرْضَ وَالسَّمَاوَاتِ الْعُلَى ٤ الرَّحْمَٰنُ عَلَى الْعَرْشِ اسْتَوَى ٥
طه ٥-١

يس ١ وَالْقُرْآنِ الْحَكِيمِ ٢ إِنَّكَ لَمِنَ الْمُرْسَلِينَ ٣ عَلَى صِرَاطٍ مُّسْتَقِيمٍ ٤ تَنزِيلَ الْعَزِيزِ الرَّحِيمِ ٥
يس ٥-١

وَالنَّجْمِ إِذَا هَوَى ١ مَا ضَلَّ صَاحِبُكُمْ وَمَا غَوَى ٢ وَمَا يَنطِقُ عَنِ الْهَوَى ٣ إِنْ هُوَ إِلَّا وَحْيٌ يُوحَى ٤ عَلَّمَهُ شَدِيدُ الْقُوَى ٥
النجم ٥-١

Lamar Shalaby
08-28-24

Allah's Compassion to His Prophet

While reading the Qur'an, I came across many verses directed to Prophet Muhammad (PBUH).

The great Prophet, peace be upon him, fulfilled his mission and established a Muslim state and a believing nation that was the basis for spreading Islam worldwide. And he fulfilled Allah's will to bring people out of darkness and into the light of Faith. They created a just state which laid the foundation for humanity to thrive – a chance to advance science, lead fulfilling lives, and to live in harmony with nature.

How many difficulties did the Messenger experience from the non-believers and the hypocrites? How many battles did the Prophet lead as the army commander - not hiding in the presidential palace protected by hundreds of guards.

Allah Almighty reassured his Messenger, Muhammad, peace be upon him, that He has forgiven all his previous sins and what is to come. Allah also told his Messenger that he possesses great manners and that he will be rewarded the highest reward.

Allah promised our beloved Messenger that he would one day free Makkah and promised him a good place in Jannah. Allah ordered him to be patient, to protect his salah, and to engage in remembrance of Allah day and night.

{ When God made a covenant with the prophets, He said, "Here is the Book and the wisdom which I have given you. When there comes to you a messenger fulfilling that which is with you, you must believe in him and help him. Do you then affirm this and accept the responsibility I have laid upon you in these terms?" They said, "We will affirm it." God said, "Then bear witness, and I will bear witness with you." } Al-'Imran-81

There is a story behind the painted oranges. I was serving some oranges to my young granddaughter. I asked her "Fayruz, how come that the orange juice does not spill out when we cut the orange?

She pointed at the tiny, juice-filled vesicles. I reminded her of the perfect creation of Allah (SWT).

....

Qur'anic Verses in the Painting:

{ Ta Ha (1) We have not sent the Qur'an down to you to distress you, (2) but only as an exhortation for him who fears God; (3) it is a revelation from Him who has created the earth and the high heavens, (4) the All Merciful settled on the throne. (5) To Him belongs whatever is in the heavens and whatever is on the earth, and whatever lies in between them, and all that lies under the ground. (6) Whether you speak aloud [or in a low voice], He hears all, for He knows your secrets and what is even more hidden. (7) God, there is no deity but Him. His are the most excellent names. (8) } Ta-Ha-1-8

To be continued on next pages.

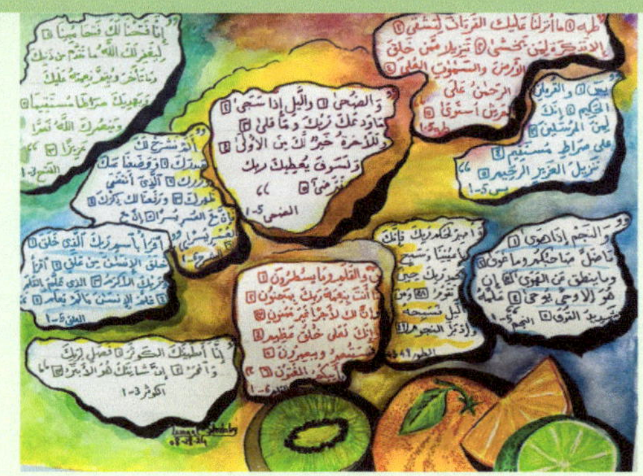

Allah's Compassion to His Prophet (Continued 1)

Other Qur'anic Verses in the Painting:

{ Ya Seen. (1) By the Qur'an, full of wisdom, (2) you are indeed one of the messengers (3) on a straight path, (4) with a revelation sent down by the Mighty One, the Merciful, (5) } Ya-Seen-1-5

{ By the setting star, (1) your companion has neither strayed nor is he misguided, (2) nor does he speak out of his own desire. (3) It [the Qur'an] is nothing but revelation sent down to him. (4) He was taught by [an angel] who is mighty in power, (5) } An-Najm-1-5

{ Have We not lifted up your heart, (1) and removed your burden (2) that weighed so heavily on your back, and (3) have We not given you high renown? (4) So, surely with every hardship there is ease; (5) surely, with every hardship there is ease. (6) } Ash-Sharh-1-6

{ So wait patiently for the Judgement of your Lord -- you are certainly under Our watchful eye. And glorify and celebrate the praises of your Lord when you rise up [from your sleep]. (48) Extol His glory at night, and at the setting of the stars. (49) } At-Tur-48&49

{ Nun. By the pen, and all that they write! (1) By the grace of your Lord, you are not a mad man. (2) Most surely, you will have a never-ending reward. (3) For you are truly of a sublime character. (4) Soon you will see, as will they, (5) which of you is a prey to madness. (6) } Al-Qalam-1-6

{ By the glorious morning light; (1) and by the night when it darkens, (2) your Lord has not forsaken you, nor is He displeased with you, (3) and the Hereafter will indeed be better for you than the present life; (4) soon you will be gratified with what your Lord will give you. (5) Did He not find you orphaned and shelter you? (6) Did He not find you wandering, and give you guidance? (7) Did He not find you in want, and make you free from want? (8) Therefore do not treat the orphan with harshness, (9) and do not chide the one who asks for help; (10) but proclaim the blessings of your Lord. (11)} Adh-Dhuha-1-11

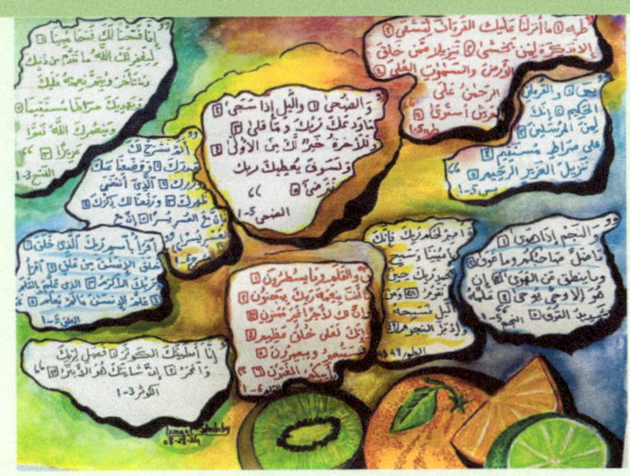

Allah's Compassion to His Prophet (Continued 2)

Other Qur'anic Verses in the Painting:

{ Truly, We have granted you a clear victory (1) so that God may forgive you your past and future sins and complete His favor to you and guide you to a straight path, (2) and so that God might bestow on you His mighty help. (3) } Al-Fath-1-3

{ Indeed, We have granted you O Prophet abundant goodness. (1) So pray and sacrifice to your Lord alone. (2) Only the one who hates you is truly cut off from any goodness. (3) } Al-Kauther-1-3

{ Read! In the name of your Lord, who created: (1) created man from a clot [of blood]. (2) Read! Your Lord is the Most Bountiful One (3) who taught by the pen, (4) taught man what he did not know. (5) } Al-'Alaq-1-5

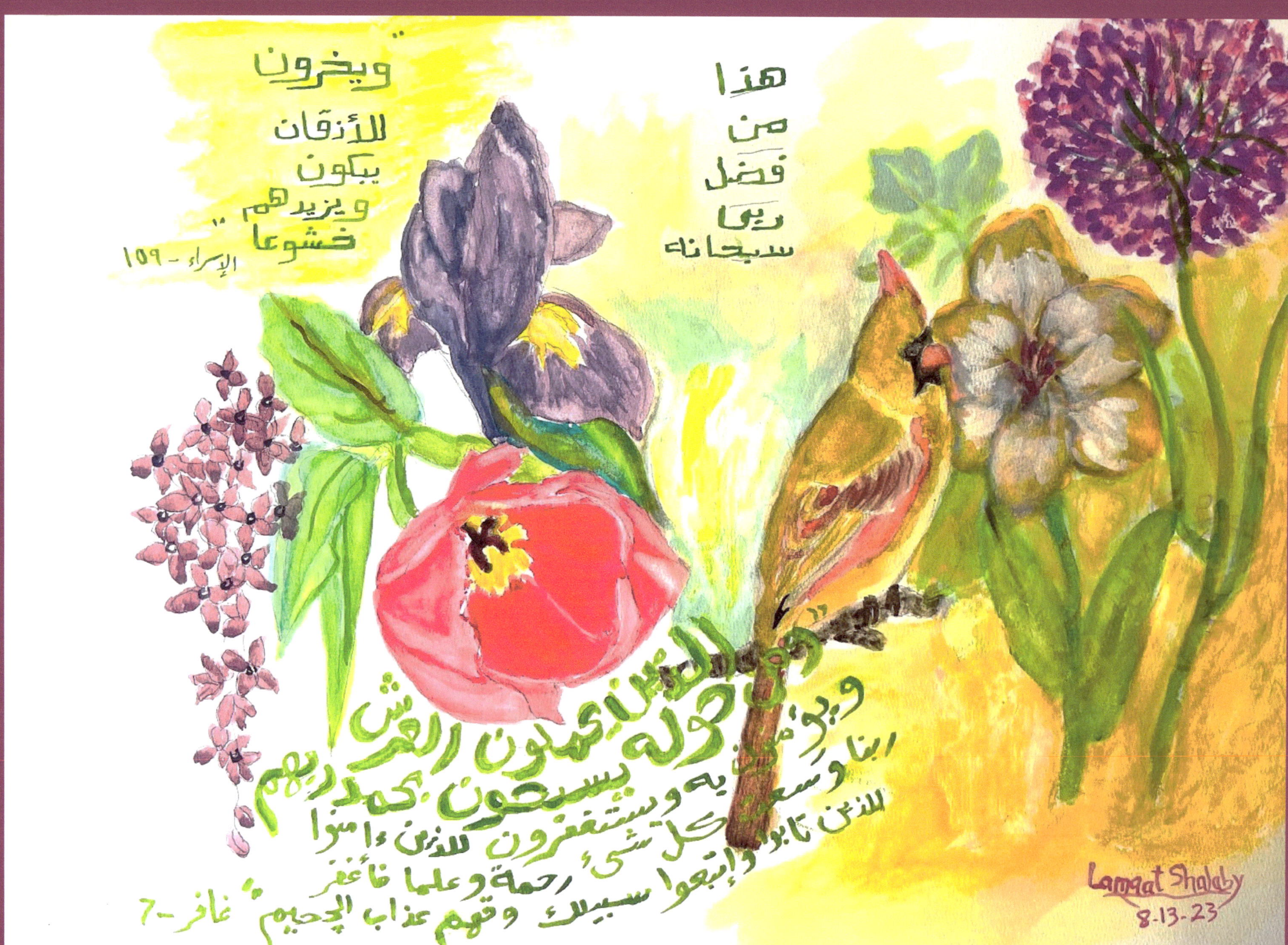

هذا
من
فضل
ربي
سبحانه

ويخرون
للأذقان
يبكون
ويزيدهم
خشوعا "
الإسراء - ١٥٩

وهو الذي
ويقيمون حوله ويحملون العرش الذين
ابنا وسعت يسبحون بحمد ربهم
الذين تابوا كل شيء ويستغفرون للذين آمنوا
رحمة وعلما فاغفر واتبعوا سبيلك وقهم عذاب الجحيم غافر - ٧

Lammat Shalaby
8-13-23

The Throne's Carriers

What a treat that Allah granted all mankind - the variety of flowers: the color, the shape, and the texture, in addition to the beautiful, fragrant scents. Some look like a gorgeous butterfly, such as the Iris. Others are delicate and beautifully scented as Jasmine and Gardenia. They are all beautiful to look at and make us happy.

The perfect creation of Allah enables the butterflies and insects like honey bees to feed on the flower nectar, which will in turn pollinate the plants. The bees make honey to feed their young ones and also a wonderful treat for humans. Praise be to Allah and His perfect creation. His creations are always beautiful, useful and durable. Manmade things are imperfect due to our greed for profit, our lack of patience, and our limited knowledge.

Let us now reflect on the great moment on the Day of Judgement when the angels will praise Allah Almighty and will ask Him to forgive the believers. What a sight...

{ Those who bear the Throne, and those who are around it, glorify their Lord with His praise, and believe in Him. They ask forgiveness for those who believe, saying, "Our Lord, You embrace all things in mercy and knowledge. Forgive those who turn to You and follow Your path. Save them from the punishment of Hell(7) and admit them, Lord, to the Eternal Garden You have promised to them, together with their righteous ancestors, spouses, and offspring: You alone are the Almighty; the All Wise. (8) Protect them from all evil deeds: those You protect from evil deeds will receive Your mercy -- that is the supreme success." (9) } Ghafir-7-9

....

Other Qur'anic Verses in the Painting:

{ We have revealed the Qur'an with the truth, and with the truth it has come down. We have sent you forth only to give good news and to give warning -- (105) We have revealed the Qur'an bit by bit so that you may recite it to the people slowly and with deliberation. We have imparted it by gradual revelation. (106) Say to them, "You may believe in it or not. Those to whom knowledge had been revealed, fall on their faces in prostration when it is recited, (107) and say, "Glory to our Lord! Our Lord's promise is bound to be fulfilled." (108) They fall down upon their faces weeping, and [the Qur'an] increases their humility." (109) } Al-Israa'-105-109

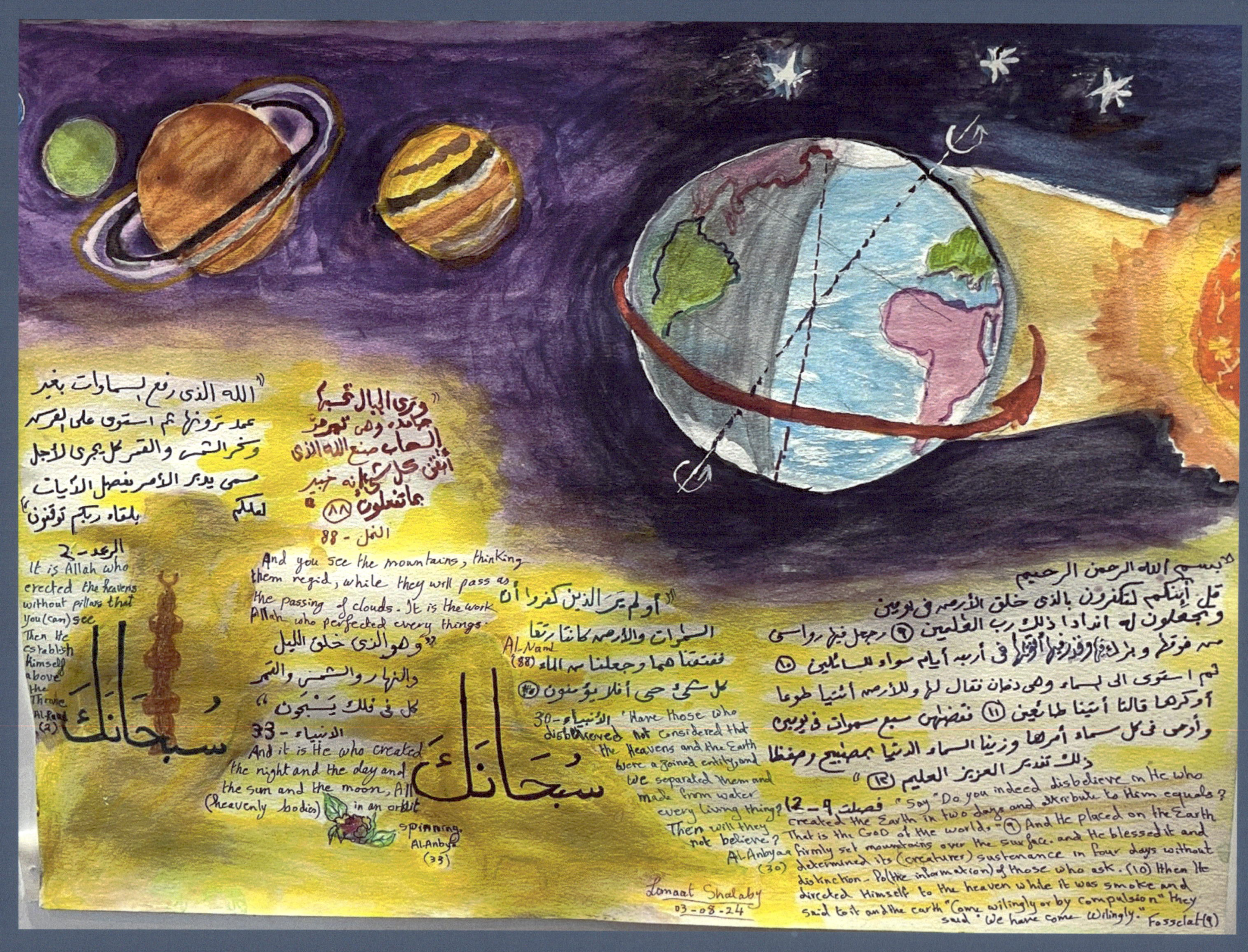

It is Allah who erected the heavens without pillars that you (can) see
Then He establish Himself above the Throne
Al-Raad (2)

And you see the mountains, thinking them regid, while they will pass as the passing of clouds. It is the work Allah who perfected every things.
Al-Naml (88)

And it is He who created the night and the day and the sun and the moon, All (heavenly bodies) in an orbit spinning.
Al-Anbya (33)

Have those who not considered that the Heavens and the Earth were a joined entity, and we separated them and made from water every living thing? Then will they not believe?
Al-Anbya (30)

"Say "Do you indeed disbelieve on He who created the Earth in two days and attribute to Him equals? That is the GoD of the world. (9) And He placed on the Earth firmly set mountains over the surface. and He blessed it and determined its (creatures) sustenance in four days without distinction - Fo(the information) of those who ask. (10) Then He directed Himself to the heaven while it was smoke and said to it and the earth "Come wilingly or by compulsion" they said "We have come Wilingly."
Fosselat (9)

Lamaat Shalaby
03-08-24

The Creator of the Universe

In the Holy Qur'an, Allah Almighty informs us about how He created the Heavens and the Earth from one origin.

{ Say, "What ! Do you indeed deny Him Who created the earth in two Days [periods] and do you set up equals with Him? He is the Lord of the Universe." (9) He placed firm mountains on the earth, and blessed it. He measured out its means of sustenance all in four Days; this is for those who ask for it. (10) Then He turned to heaven when it was smoke and said to it and to the earth, "Come willingly or unwillingly." They both said, "We come willingly," (11) and in two Days He formed seven heavens, and revealed to each heaven its functions; and We adorned the lower heaven with brilliant lamps [stars] and guarded it. That is the decree of the Almighty, the All Knowing. (12) } Fussilat-9-12

In the nineteenth century scientists proposed The Big Bang Theory. Humans finally began to understand the Truth that Allah referred to thirteen centuries earlier. Glory be to Allah, Subhanahu. Allah Almighty also informed us in the Qur'an that everything living was created from water.

{ Do not those who deny the truth see that the heavens and the earth were joined together and that We then split them asunder? And that We have made every living thing out of water? Will they still not believe?} Al-Anbiya'-30

Allah mentioned in the Qur'an that mountains on Earth are not standing still but moving smoothly like the passing of clouds.

{ You see the mountains and think they are firmly fixed. But they shall pass away as the clouds pass away. Such is the work of God, who has ordered all things to perfection: He is fully aware of what you do.} An-Naml-88

This could happen if the earth were rotating. Mankind discovered and proved that Earth was rotating around its own axis more than twelve centuries after the Qur'an was revealed to Prophet Muhammad (PBUH).

Recently, scientists suggested that the universe is expanding based on their observations and research. This is exactly what Allah (SWT) told us more than 1400 years ago in the Qur'an;

{ We built the universe with great might, and We are certainly expanding it } Adh-Dhariyat-47   **Ref.3**

And He created the night and the day, the sun and the moon. Each follows its own orbit for a specified term.

{ It is He who created the night and the day, and the sun and the moon, each gliding in its orbit. } Al-Anbiya'-33

It took humans hundreds of years to advance their science enough to study and understand these facts. And yet, they were revealed over a thousand years ago. This is proof that the Qur'an is a Divine Book from Allah the Almighty – the Creator and all-Knower.

And when humans were created, they were created in the best form.

{ We have indeed created man in the best of form } At-Tin - 4

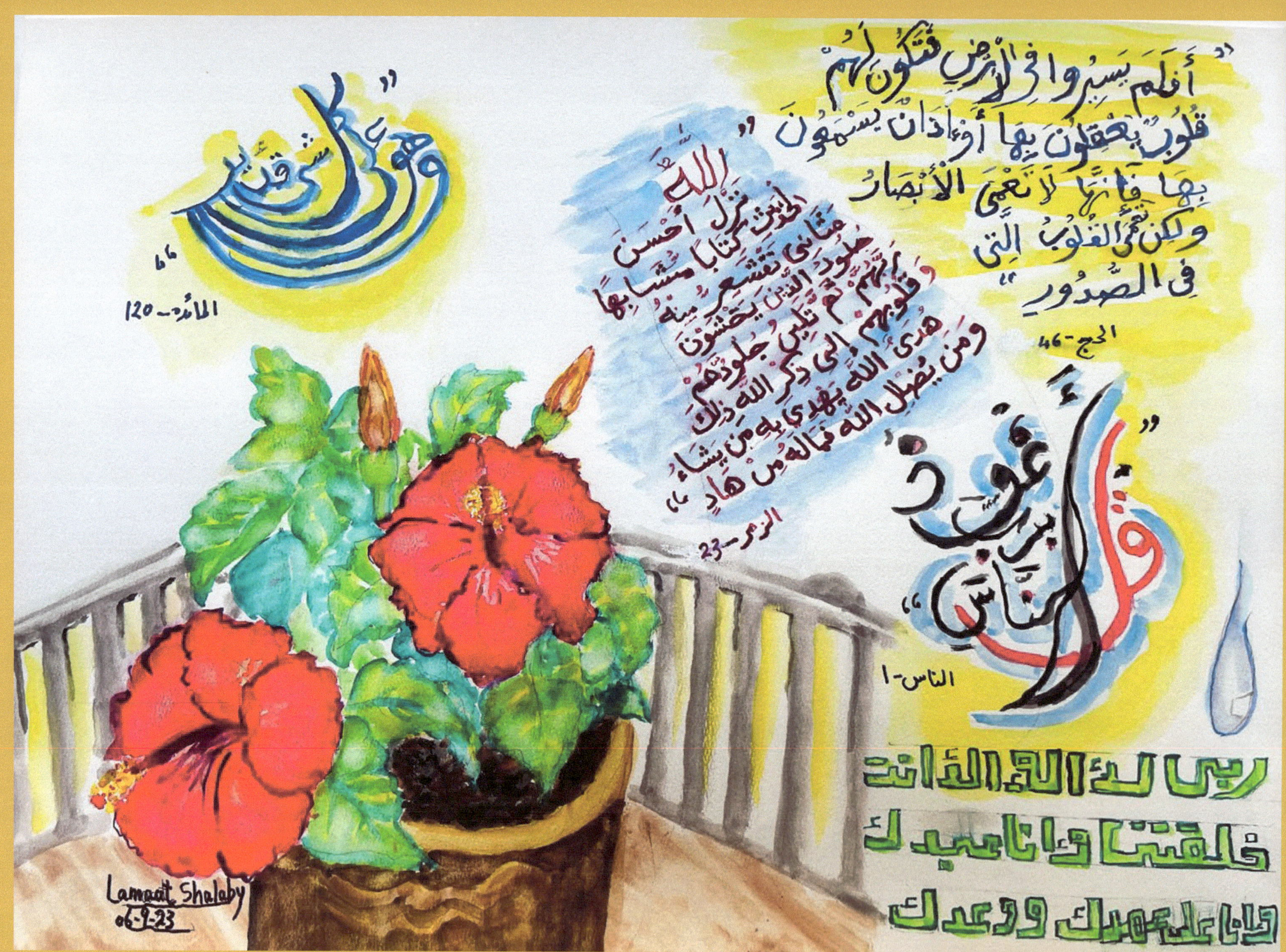
"أَفَلَمْ يَسِيرُوا فِي الْأَرْضِ فَتَكُونَ لَهُمْ قُلُوبٌ يَعْقِلُونَ بِهَا أَوْ آذَانٌ يَسْمَعُونَ بِهَا فَإِنَّهَا لَا تَعْمَى الْأَبْصَارُ وَلَكِنْ تَعْمَى الْقُلُوبُ الَّتِي فِي الصُّدُورِ"
الحج - ٤٦
"وَهُوَ عَلَى كُلِّ شَيْءٍ قَدِيرٌ"
المائدة - ١٢٠
"اللَّهُ نَزَّلَ أَحْسَنَ الْحَدِيثِ كِتَابًا مُتَشَابِهًا مَثَانِيَ تَقْشَعِرُّ مِنْهُ جُلُودُ الَّذِينَ يَخْشَوْنَ رَبَّهُمْ ثُمَّ تَلِينُ جُلُودُهُمْ وَقُلُوبُهُمْ إِلَى ذِكْرِ اللَّهِ ذَلِكَ هُدَى اللَّهِ يَهْدِي بِهِ مَنْ يَشَاءُ وَمَنْ يُضْلِلِ اللَّهُ فَمَا لَهُ مِنْ هَادٍ"
الزمر - ٢٣
"قُلْ أَعُوذُ بِرَبِّ النَّاسِ"
الناس - ١
رَبِّ لَا إِلَهَ إِلَّا أَنْتَ خَلَقْتَنِي وَأَنَا عَبْدُكَ وَأَنَا عَلَى عَهْدِكَ وَوَعْدِكَ
Lamaat Shalaby
06-9-23

The Miracle of The Qur'an

Glory be to Allah, how beautiful is the blessing of His words, the Holy Qur'an. If all trees in this world were pens and the water of all the seas and oceans were ink, they will not be enough to write Allah's words, as Allah (SWT) said in the following verse:

{ If all the trees on earth were pens, and the sea [were] ink, with seven [more] seas added to it, the words of God would not be exhausted: for, truly, God is Almighty and Wise. } Luqman-27

One of the miracles of the Qur'an is that Allah Almighty made it accessible to every person and it fits everybody's knowledge and ability. The Qur'an addresses all people: the believers, the nonbelievers, and the people of the book, men and women, young and old.

The Qur'an deals with everything that is important to mankind. If a person needs divine guidance in any important matter, he will find it in Allah's honorable book, the Qur'an. The Qur'an addresses all important aspects of human life. **Ref.4**

If any reader opens the first two pages of the Qur'an, he will find the core of the faith and the divine message in them, accurately and simply presented. Even if a person stops at those first two pages, he will have read the call of Islam and the message of all the Prophets.

On the first page, Surah Al-Fatiha starts with praising Allah, followed by a reminder that Allah Ta'ala is the Most Gracious, the Most Merciful. Allah is in charge of the Day of Judgment and He is the only One we worship. It is then followed by a dua'a (supplication) to be on the straight path leading to Jannah which is the reward of the believers, and not the path of the cursed ones nor those who have gone astray.

{ All praise is due to God, the Lord of the Universe; (2) the Beneficent, the Merciful; (3) Lord of the Day of Judgement. (4) You alone we worship, and to You alone we turn for help. (5) Guide us to the straight path: (6) the path of those You have blessed; not of those who have incurred Your wrath, nor of those who have gone astray. (7) } Al-Fatiha-1-7

The second page, which is the beginning of Surah Al-Baqara, confirms to the reader that this Book is no doubt the authentic word of Allah, and it is the guide for the people who fear Allah Almighty. The winners are the believers who pray, offer the zakat and spend from what Allah Ta'ala has granted them to the poor and needy.

{ Alif Lam Mim. (1) This is the Book; there is no doubt in it. It is a guide for those who are mindful of God, (2) who believe in the unseen, and are steadfast in prayer, and spend out of what We have provided them with; (3) those who believe in the revelation sent down to you and in what was sent before you, and firmly believe in the life to come -- (4) they are the people who are rightly following their Lord and it is they who shall be successful. (5) } Al-Baqara-1-5

To be continued on next pages.

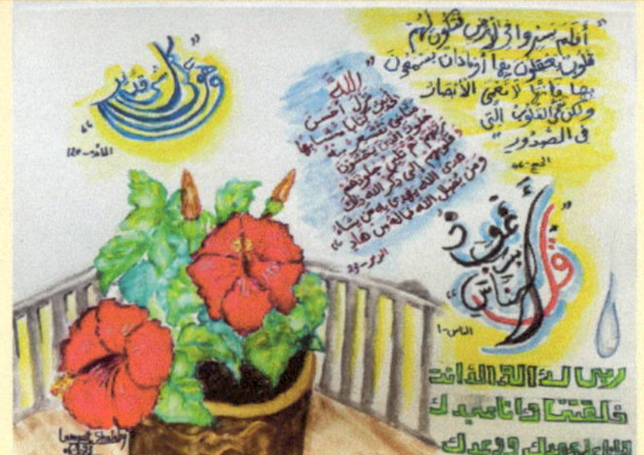

The Miracle of The Qur'an (Continued 1)

Examples of different subjects in the Qur'an (not as a comprehensive list):

* Faith is in Surah Al-Baqara, Al-'Imran, Al-An'aam, Al- Mo'menoon, and As-Saff

* The Qur'an book is in Surah Al-Baqara, Al-'Imran, Al-Hashr, Luqman, Ta-Ha, and Al-Hijr

* Isa, peace be upon him, and Maryam, peace be upon her, are in Surah Al-Baqara, Al-'Imran, Al-Ma'eda, Maryam, Ash-Shura, and Al-Ahzab

* Family affairs such as marriage, divorce and raising children, are in Surah Al-Baqara, At-Talaq, and Luqman

* The just laws of inheritance in Surah An-Nisaa'

* Financial transactions in Surah Al-Baqara, An-Nisaa', Al-Ma'eda, and Al-Mutaffifin.

*Laws of war, defense: Surah Al-Anfal, At-Tawba, and Al-Baqara.

* Morality and manners: in Surah Al-Hujraat, Luqman, and Al-Ahzab.

* Fasting, hajj, halal food, wine, gambling and riba (usury), you will find them in Surah Al-Baqara and Al-An'aam

* The verses of the miracles of Allah's creation are found in Surah An-Nahl, Ar-Rahman, and Al-Waqui'a

*The unseen and beyond: is in Al-Israa', Al-'Imran, Al-A'raf, An-Najm, Al-Qamar and Ar-Rahman.

* Stories of the Prophets are mentioned more than once from different aspects in Surah Al-Baqara, Al-Ma'eda, Al-'Imran, Ibrahim, Hud, Nuh, Yunus, Youssef, Ta-Ha, and Muhammad.

All of the Qur'an's verses complement and confirm each other, which confirms that the Qur'an was revealed from One source, Allah, the Almighty.

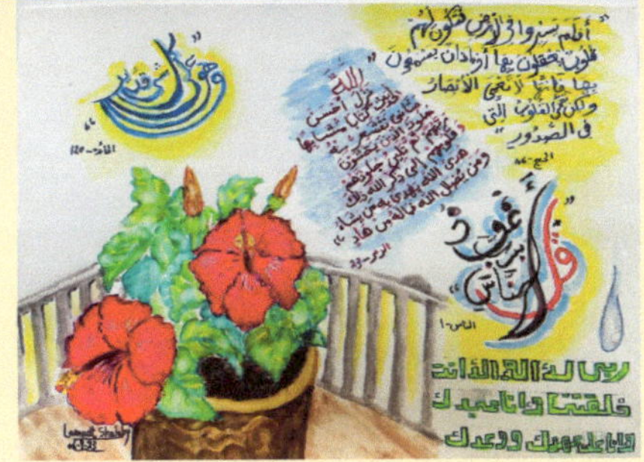

The Miracle of The Qur'an (Continued 2)

....

Other Qur'anic Verses in the Painting:

{ God has sent down the best Message: a Scripture that is consimilar and oft-repeated: that causes the skins of those in awe of their Lord to creep. Then their skins and their hearts soften at the mention of God: such is God's guidance. He bestows it upon whoever He will; but no one can guide those whom God leaves to stray. } Az-Zumar-23

{ Have these people not traveled through the land to make their hearts understand and let their ears hear; the truth is that it is not the eyes that are blind but the hearts that are in the chests that are blinded. } Al-Hajj-46

{ Say, "I seek refuge in the Lord of people, } An-Nas-1

{ The kingdom of the heavens and the earth and everything in them belongs to God: He has power over all things. } Al-Ma'eda-120

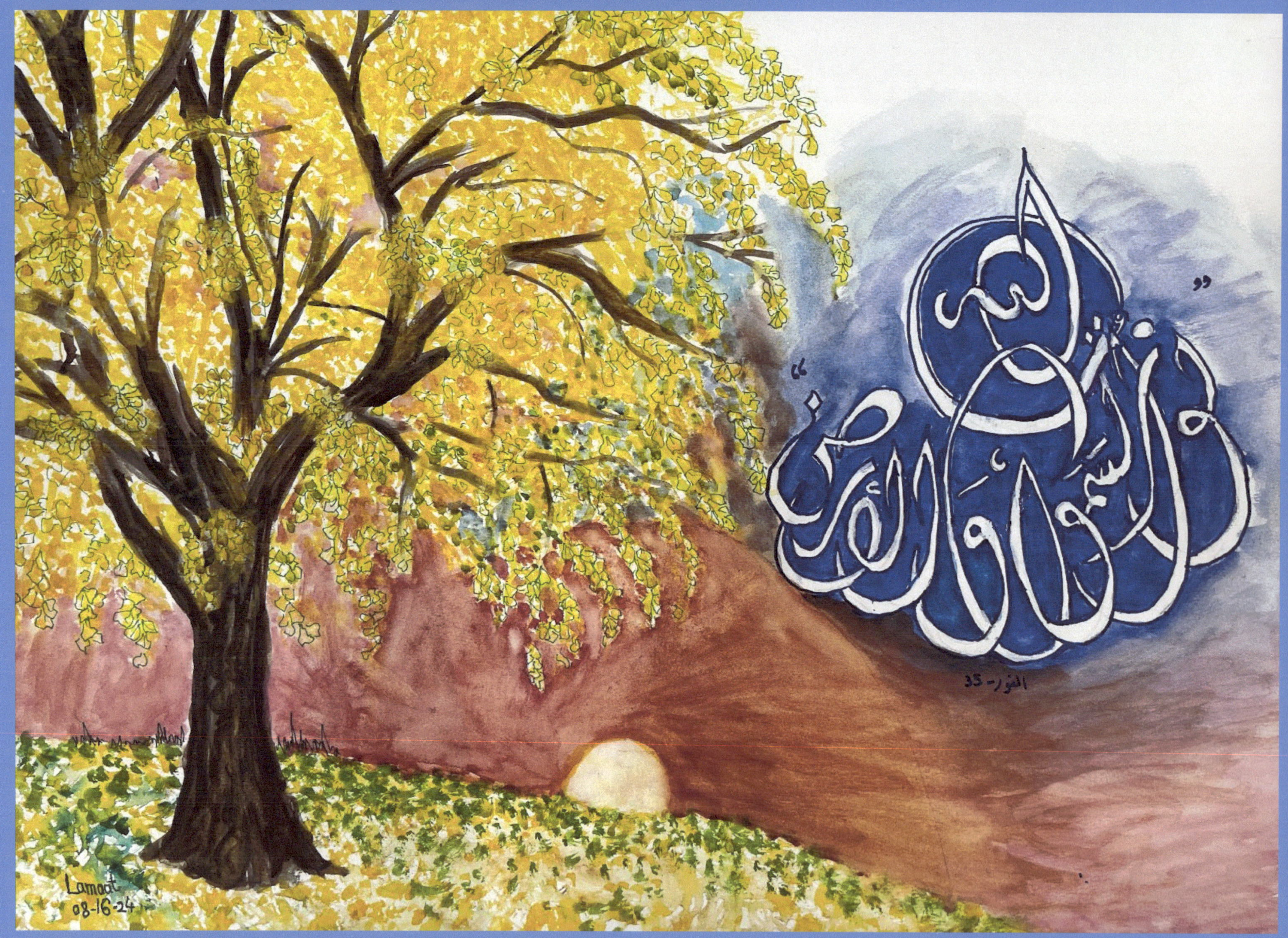

اللهُ نُورُ السَّمَاوَاتِ وَالْأَرْضِ
النور - 35

Longing for Allah

I always feel serene when I recite { Allah is the light of the heavens and the earth... } and I repeat { Noor upon Noor (light upon light) }.

Allah Almighty has given the believers so many blessings in this world and has blessed them with the Qur'an. He will grant them Jannah and they will look towards Him in Jannah, as Allah, Almighty said:

{ Some faces will be radiant on that Day, (22) looking towards their Lord; (23) } Al-Qiyama-22&23

And in the Qur'an, Allah, Ta'ala said:

{ There they shall have all that they desire, and there is even more with Us. } Qaf-35

" More " here is: Looking at Allah as explained by Ali and Anas bin Malik, may Allah be pleased with them.

Allah, Almighty also said:

{ Those who do good deeds shall have a good reward and more besides... } Yunus-26

The good reward is Jannah and "More" here is to look at Allah, as explained by the Messenger, may Allah's prayers and peace be upon him.

As Muslim narrated in his Sahih (266) from Suhaib, may Allah be pleased with him, from the Prophet, may Allah's prayers and peace be upon him, he said: When the people of Jannah enter Jannah, he said: Allah Almighty says: Do you want something more? I shall grant you. They say: "Didn't You fill our faces with Noor, and allow us to enter Paradise and save us from the Hell fire? The Prophet said, so the veil is revealed. So they (the people of Paradise) are not given anything more rewarding to them than looking at their Lord Almighty, which is the extra reward.

Then he recited { Those who do good deeds shall have a good reward and more besides... } Yunus-26

....

Qur'anic Verse in the Painting:

{ Allah is the light of the heavens and the earth. His light may be compared to a niche containing a lamp, the lamp inside a crystal of star-like brilliance lit from a blessed olive tree, neither of the east nor of the west. The [luminous] oil is as if ready to burn without even touching it. Light upon light; God guides to His light whom He will. God draws such comparisons for mankind; God has full knowledge of everything. } An-Noor-35

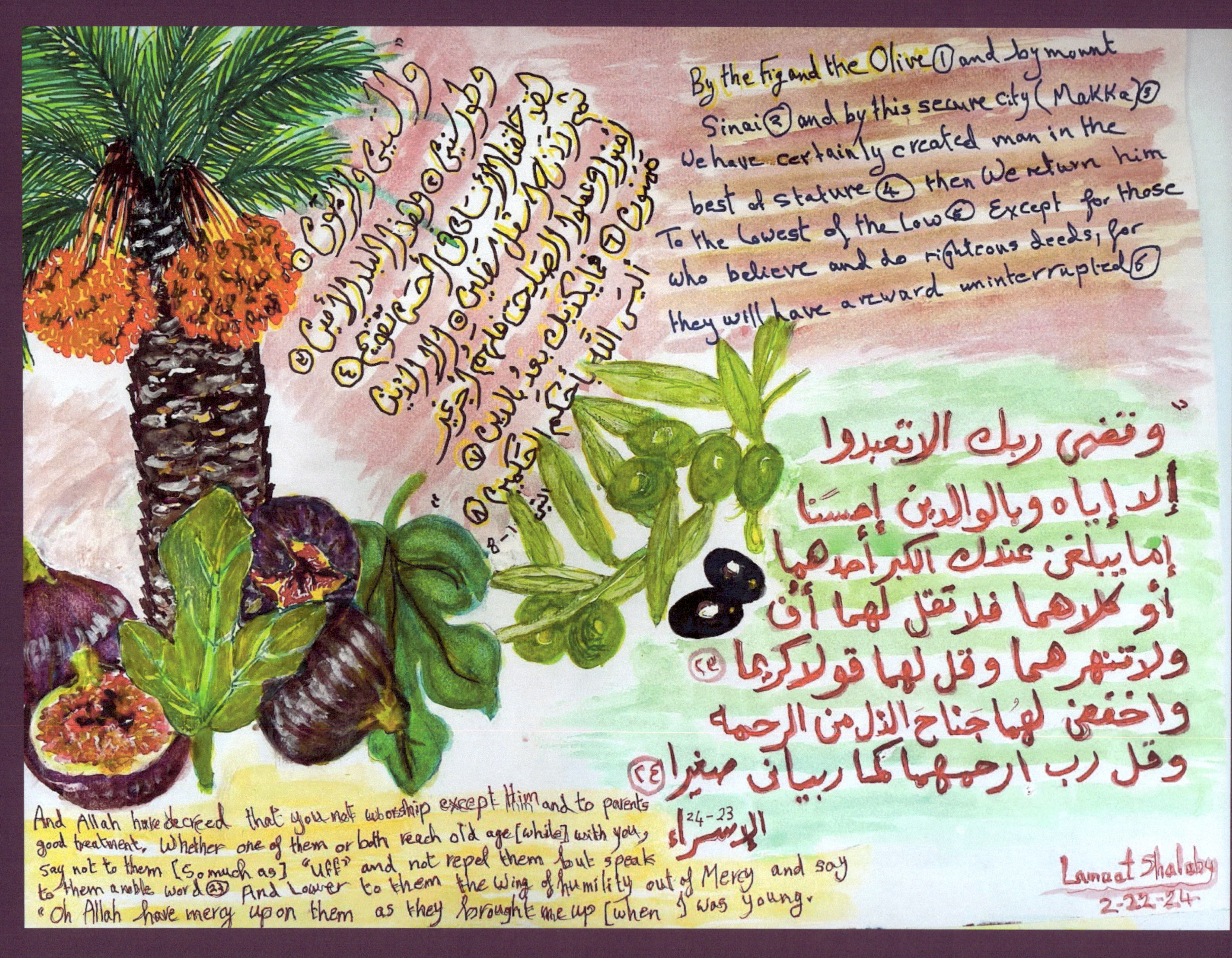
By the Fig and the Olive ① and by mount
Sinai ② and by this secure city (Makka) ③
We have certainly created man in the
best of stature ④ then We return him
To the Lowest of the Low ⑤ Except for those
who believe and do righteous deeds, for
they will have a reward uninterrupted ⑥

وقضى ربك الا تعبدوا
إلا إياه وبالوالدين إحسانا
إما يبلغن عندك الكبر أحدهما
أو كلاهما فلا تقل لهما أف
ولا تنهرهما وقل لهما قولا كريما ㉓
واخفض لهما جناح الذل من الرحمه
وقل رب ارحمهما كما ربياني صغيرا ㉔
الإسراء 24-23

And Allah have decreed that you not worship except Him and to parents
good treatment, Whether one of them or both reach old age [while] with you,
say not to them [so much as] "Uff" and not repel them but speak
to them a noble word ㉓ And Lower to them the wing of humility out of Mercy and say
"Oh Allah have mercy upon them as they brought me up [when] I was young.

Lamaat Shalaby
2-22-24

Mankind is Created in the Best Form

I read Surah At-Teen in my salah a lot. It starts with Allah SWT, swearing by the fig and the olive, which might be a reference to Palestine where many Prophets were dwelling including Prophet Isa, peace be upon him, then Mount Sinai, a reference to Prophet Musa, peace be upon him, and then by the blessed city of Makkah in reference to the seal of the Prophets, Muhammad, peace be upon him.

{ By the Fig and the Olive, (1) and by Mount Sinai, (2) and by this secure land, (3) } At-Tin-1-3

Then Allah, the Creator, the most Merciful, tells us about mankind. Allah (SWT) has created him in the best form and has given him the freedom to choose. Mankind can choose the path of faith and good deeds or the path of no faith and bad deeds. This is the truth that no human being can deny because it is from Allah the Most Wise.

{ We have indeed created man in the best of mold, (4) then We cast him down as the lowest of the low, (5) except for those who believe and do good deeds -- theirs shall be an unending reward! (6) What then after this, can make you deny the Last Judgment? (7) Is not God the greatest of the judges? (8) } At-Tin-4-8

Caring for the parents is one of the most important commandments that Allah has commanded us after the first commandment, which is worshiping Him alone. And caring for parents has special importance, especially in their stage of aging and physical and mental weakness. It is certain that if parents raise their children to know Allah, these children will treat their parents well. On the other hand, if the child does not grow up knowing Allah, there is no guarantee that he will be righteous with his parents.

{ Your Lord has commanded that you should worship none but Him, and show kindness to your parents. If either or both of them attain old age with you, say no word of contempt to them and do not rebuke them, but always speak gently to them (23) and treat them with humility and tenderness and say, "Lord, be merciful to them both, as they raised me up when I was little." (24) } Al-Israa'-23&24

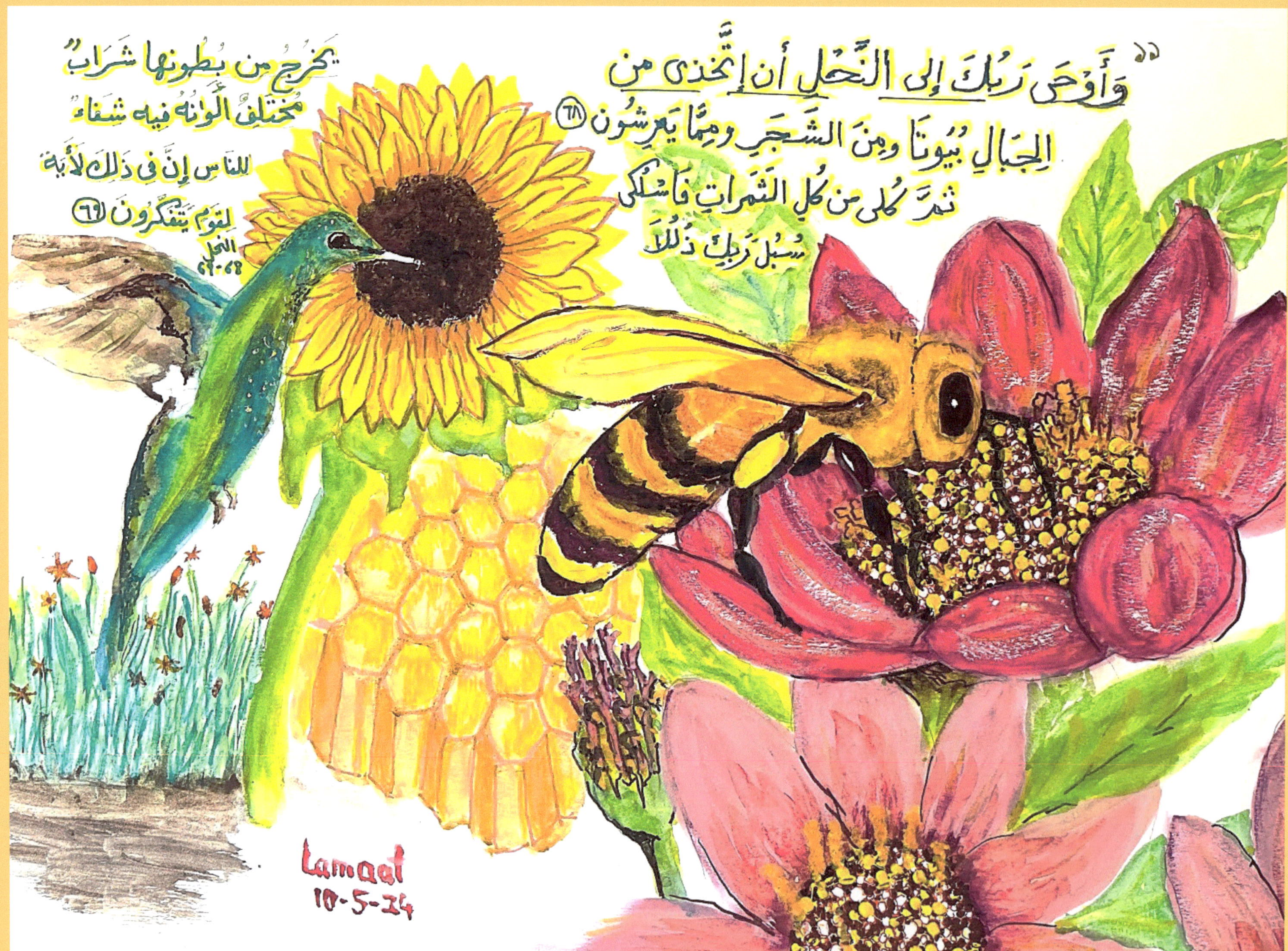

وَأَوْحَى رَبُّكَ إِلَى النَّحْلِ أَنِ اتَّخِذِي مِنَ الْجِبَالِ بُيُوتًا وَمِنَ الشَّجَرِ وَمِمَّا يَعْرِشُونَ ۝ ثُمَّ كُلِي مِن كُلِّ الثَّمَرَاتِ فَاسْلُكِي سُبُلَ رَبِّكِ ذُلُلًا
يَخْرُجُ مِن بُطُونِهَا شَرَابٌ مُّخْتَلِفٌ أَلْوَانُهُ فِيهِ شِفَاءٌ لِّلنَّاسِ إِنَّ فِي ذَلِكَ لَآيَةً لِّقَوْمٍ يَتَفَكَّرُونَ ۝
النحل ٦٨-٦٩
lamaal
10-5-24

Allah's Directive to the Honeybees

{ Your Lord inspired the bee, saying, "Make your homes in the mountains, in the trees, and also in the structures which men erect. (68) Then feed on every kind of fruit, and follow the trodden paths of your Lord." From its belly comes a drink with different colors which provides healing for mankind. Indeed, in this there is a sign for people who give thought. (69) } An-Nahl-68&69

Glory be to You, Allah, the All-Knowing, the Wise. When we read these verses, we feel Allah's mercy and His gift to humanity. Bees have been created to make us honey of all kinds with its sweet taste and nutritional and therapeutic benefits.

Allah Almighty has told us in the Qur'an fourteen centuries ago what science has recently revealed about the miracle of the bee's life and its important role in the manufacturing of honey and the process of pollinating plants.   **Ref.5**

Allah Almighty created the bees and mentioned in the Qur'an that He revealed to them where to live, what to eat, how to communicate together, and how to find their way to the cell. Allah taught the bees to absorb the nectar of the flowers and to make and store honey in their honeycomb cells. These cells, with a distinctive hexagonal shape, are built from beeswax secreted by specialized bees for this task. Allah taught bees to build their homes (beehives) in the mountains, on trees, and in man-made cells. Bees can build their homes in a large range of temperatures, altitudes, and quality of air. It may indicate that those factors affect the composition and the quality of the honey. Perhaps the mention of the order may indicate that the honey of the mountains is the best of them medically (such as the famous Manuka honey) and then honey from the tree cells, then the honey from man-made wooden cells. Science has recently proven this to be true. Verse 69 of Surah An-Nahl included: "Then feed on every kind of fruit"

It may refer to the importance of the bee feeding on the nectar of all fruit tree flowers to pollinate them and enable them to bear fruit.

The verse that follows immediately afterward in Surah An-Nahl refers to aging and mental deterioration.

{ God created you; then He shall cause you to die: and some shall have their lives prolonged to abject old age, ceasing to know anything after once having had knowledge. God is all knowing and powerful. } An-Nahl-70

How wonderful would it be to discover a type of honey that can treat aging and memory loss. Allah knows best.

Expert beekeepers recommend that a shady, south-facing beehive is ideal for beekeepers living in the northern hemisphere. A shady, north-facing beehive is best for beekeepers in the southern hemisphere. This will provide the honeybees with a warm, solar-heated porch from which the bees can take off and land all year around. **Ref.6**

It is amazing that this choice corresponds to the direction of the Qibla (Kaaba) for the five prayers prescribed by Allah Almighty in the Qur'an. Glory be to Him.

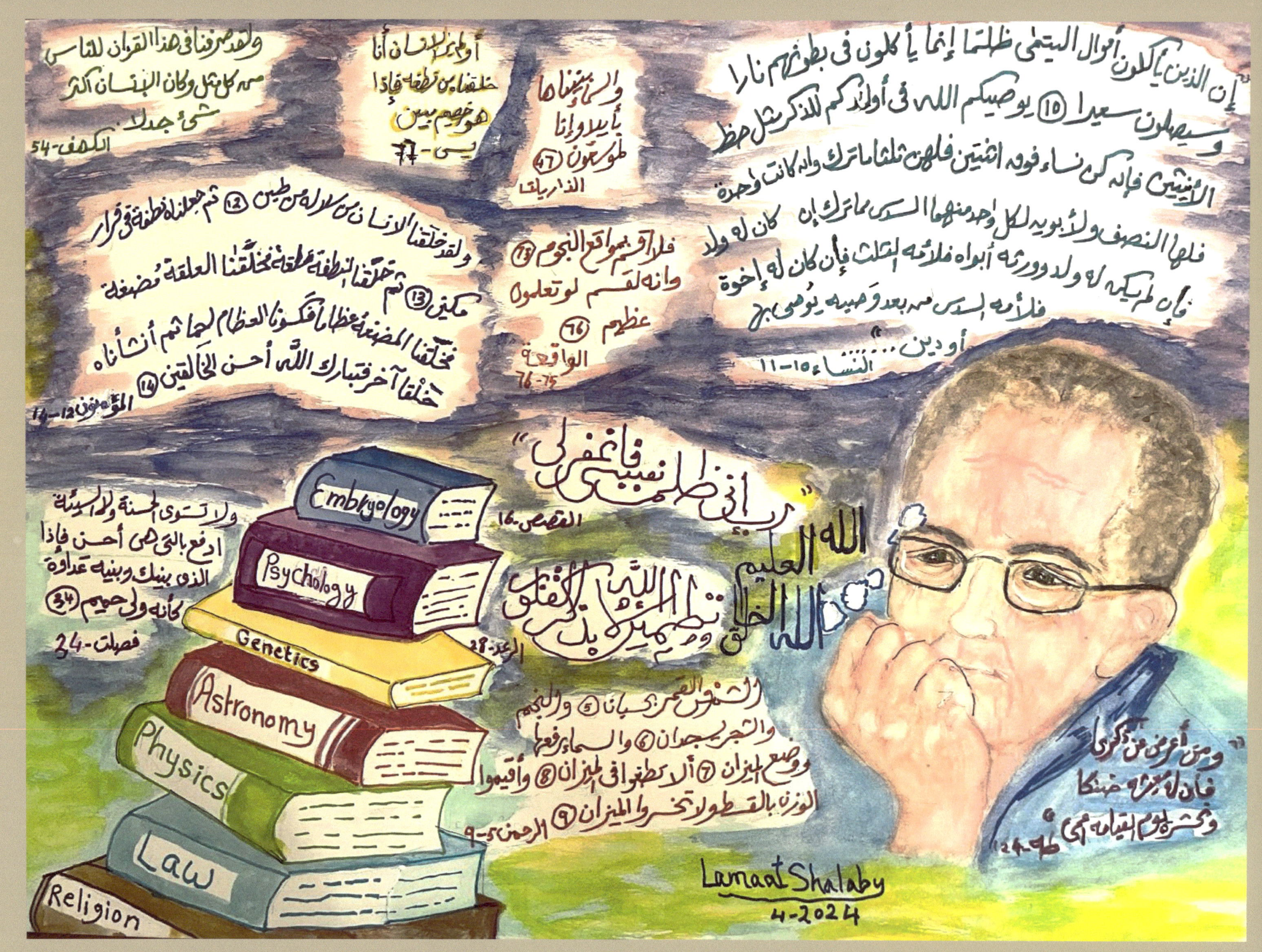

Embryology
Psychology
Genetics
Astronomy
Physics
Law
Religion
Lamaat Shalaby
4-2024

The Arrogant Human

I am a scientist who appreciates the perfect wisdom behind all of Allah's creations. I am always surprised that when mankind discovers one of the physical laws that Allah (SWT) endows in His universe for our benefit, they will glorify themselves as if they created it. They never recognize that Allah is the Creator and that perfection is His.

I wish scientific books will have an appreciation statement in the introduction stating that this is an ongoing human effort to discover the perfect laws of Allah.

The few Qur'anic verses posted in this painting are just a few examples of the endless references in Allah's Book, the Qur'an, to the laws of physics and scientific facts to be discovered in the future by mankind.

Allah Ta'ala knows that mankind will discover many advances in science because Allah has created humans with the capacity to think, learn, and discover.

Just one example is the description of how the embryo develops in the mother's womb in Surah Al- Mu'menoon verses 12-14 and Surah Al-Hajj verse 5.

{ We created man from an essence of clay, (12) then We placed him as a drop of fluid in a safe place, (13) then We developed that drop into a clinging form, and We developed that form into a lump of flesh, and We developed that lump into bones, and clothed the bones with flesh. Then We brought him into being as a new creation, glory be to God, the best of creators, (14) } Al-Mu'menoon-12-14

{ O people! If you are in doubt about the Resurrection, remember that We first created you from dust, then from a sperm drop, then from clotted blood, then a lump of flesh, both shaped and unshaped, so that We might manifest to you [Our power]. We cause what We will to stay in the womb for an appointed time, then We bring you forth as infants and then We cause you to grow and reach full growth. Then, some of you will pass away early in life, while some of you will reach extreme old age in which they will know nothing of what they once knew. You see the earth, dead and barren, but no sooner do We send down rain upon it than it begins to stir and swell, and produce every kind of luxuriant vegetation: (5) } Al-Hajj-5

We must mention here that Allah, the One and Only, has assured us at the beginning of Surah Al-Baqara, that the Qur'an is His true words and is beyond any doubt. And Allah Almighty promised us that He is the One who will protect the Qur'an from any loss or distortion.

{ This is the Book; there is no doubt in it. It is a guide for those who are mindful of God } Al-Baqara-2

{ Do they say, "He has fabricated it?" Say, "Bring me one chapter like it. Call on whom you may besides God to help you, if what you say be true!" } Yunus-3

To be continued on next pages.

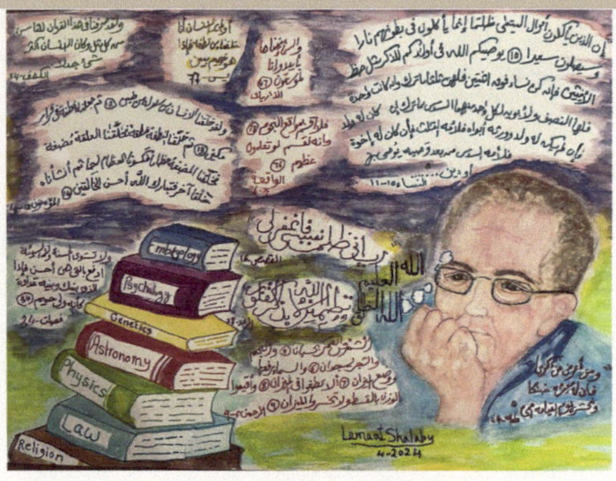

The Arrogant Human (Continued 1)

{ It is We who have sent down the Reminder and We will, most surely, safeguard it. } Al-Hijr-9

{ [Prophet], do not move your tongue too fast in your attempt to learn this revelation: (16) We Ourself shall see to its collection and recital. (17) When We have recited it, follow its words attentively; (18) and then, it will be for Us to make its meaning clear. (19) } Al-Qiyama-16-19

And in the Sahihs on the authority of Fatima, may Allah be pleased with her, and may Allah's peace and blessings be upon her father, she said: her father told her secretly that Jibreel used to review the Qur'an with him once every year, and that Jibreel reviewed it with him twice this year, and that he does not see except that the end has approached.

After all these assurances, there is no doubt in my mind that the Qur'an is the authentic word of Allah (SWT) and it is protected from any loss or distortion.

....

Other Qur'anic Verses in the Painting:

{ We have surely set forth in this Qur'an every kind of lesson for people, but humankind is the most argumentative of all beings. } Al-Kahf-54

{ Do people not see that We have created them from a sperm-drop, then—behold!—they openly challenge Us? } Ya-Seen-77

{ We built the universe with great might, and We are certainly expanding it. } Adh-Dhariyat-47

{ So I do swear by the positions of the stars— (75) and this, if only you knew, is indeed a great oath (76) } Al-Waqi'a-75&76

{ The sun and the moon travel with precision. (5) The stars and the trees bow down in submission. (6) As for the sky, He raised it high, and set the balance of justice (7) so that you do not defraud the scales. (8) Weigh with justice, and do not give short measure. (9) } Ar-Rahman-5-9

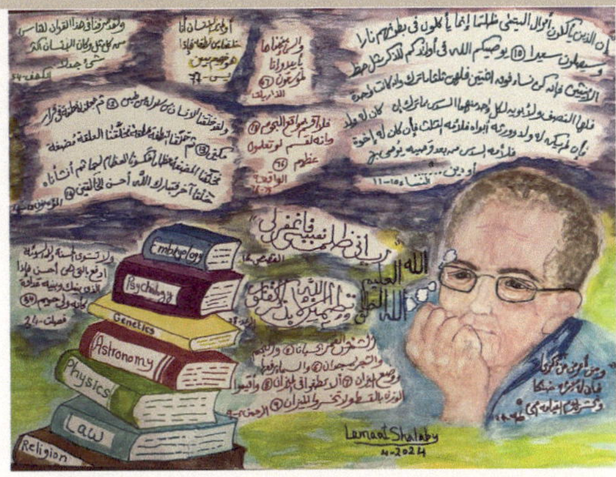

The Arrogant Human (Continued 2)

Other Qur'anic Verses in the Painting:

{ Those who believe and whose hearts find comfort in the remembrance of Allah. Surely in the remembrance of Allah do hearts find comfort }

Ar-Ra'd-28

{ But whoever turns away from My Reminder will certainly have a miserable life, then We will raise them up blind on the Day of Judgment." }

Ta-Ha-124

{ He pleaded, "My Lord! I have definitely wronged my soul, so forgive me." So He forgave him, for He is indeed the All-Forgiving, Most Merciful }
Al-Qasas-16

{ Good and evil deeds are not equal. Repel evil with what is better; then you will see that one who was once your enemy has become your dearest friend } **Fussilat-34**

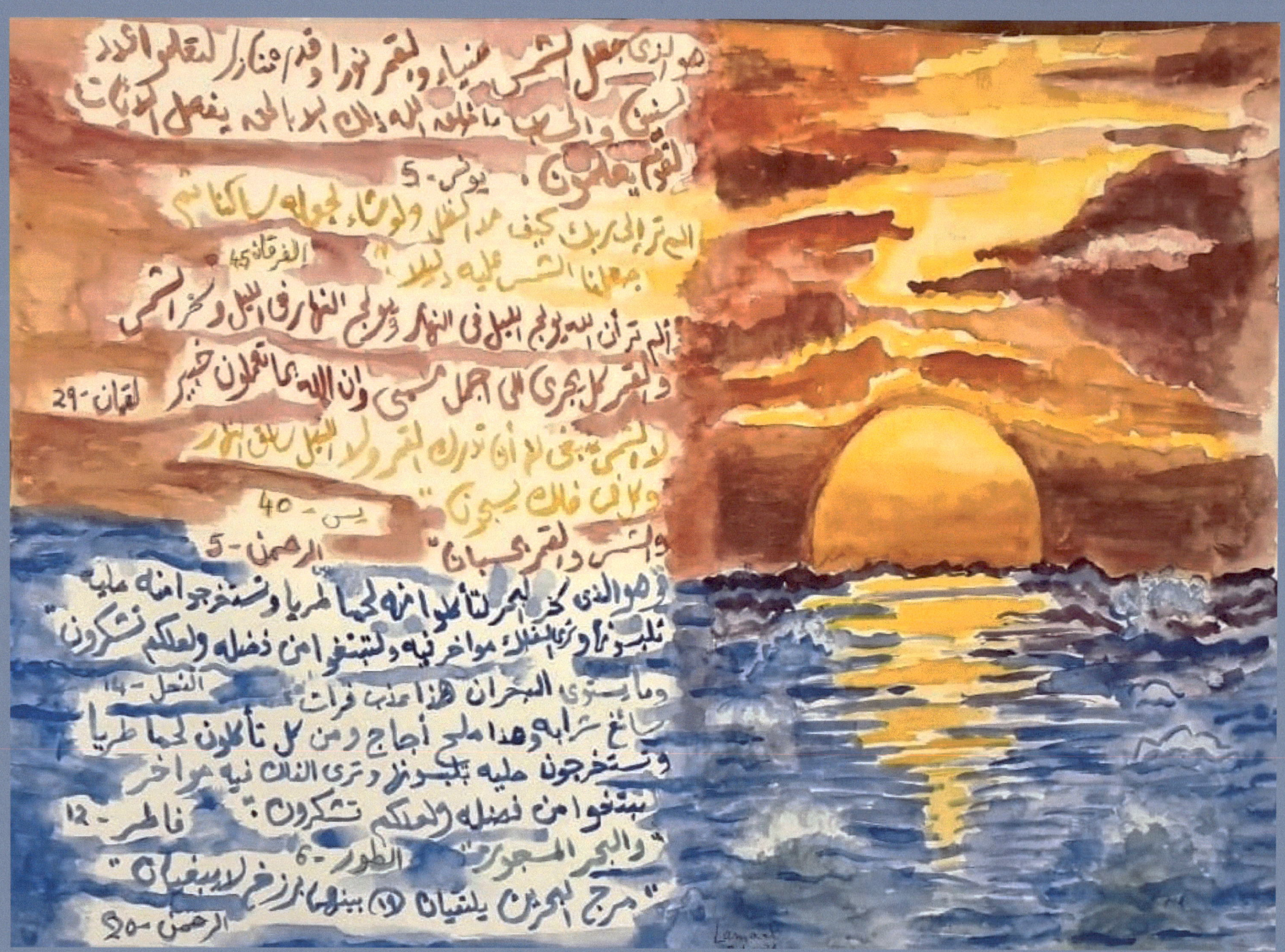

The Sunset

I was watching the sun setting on the beach with its warm, golden colors and its reflection in the clouds and on the waves. It was a beautiful scene, changing from golden yellow to orange to magenta. Darkness came after the sunset, and it was time to pray Maghrib to glorify the Creator and praise Him.

I once asked my father why there are wars, crimes, and illness all over the world. He looked at me and said "this dynamic of life is meant to be so life activities will take place and mankind will be tested to gain heaven or fall into punishment." He added that if there is no illness then there will be no medical science and medical jobs, and if there is no hunger there will be no agriculture, and so on.

....

Qur'anic Verses in the Painting:

{ He is the One Who made the sun a radiant source and the moon a reflected light, with precisely ordained phases, so that you may know the number of years and calculation of time. Allah did not create all this except for a purpose. He makes the signs clear for people of knowledge. }
Yunus-5

{ Have you not seen how your Lord extends the shadow—He could have simply made it remain still if He so willed—then We make the sun its guide } Al-Furqan-45

{ Do you not see that Allah causes the night to merge into the day and the day into the night, and has subjected the sun and the moon, each orbiting for an appointed term, and that Allah is All-Aware of what you do? } Luqman-29

{ The sun cannot overtake the moon, nor can the night outpace the day: each floats in [its own] orbit. } Ya-seen-40

{ The sun and the moon move according to a fixed reckoning; } Ar-Rahman-5

{ He merges the two bodies of fresh and salt water, (19) yet between them is a barrier they never cross. } Ar-Rahman-20

{ The two bodies of water are not alike: one is fresh, palatable, and pleasant to drink and the other is salty and bitter. Yet from them both you eat tender seafood and extract ornaments to wear. And you see the ships plowing their way through both, so you may seek His bounty and give thanks to Him. } Fatir-12

{ And He is the One Who has subjected the sea, so from it you may eat tender seafood and extract ornaments to wear. And you see the ships plowing their way through it, so you may seek His bounty and give thanks to Him. } An-Nahl-14

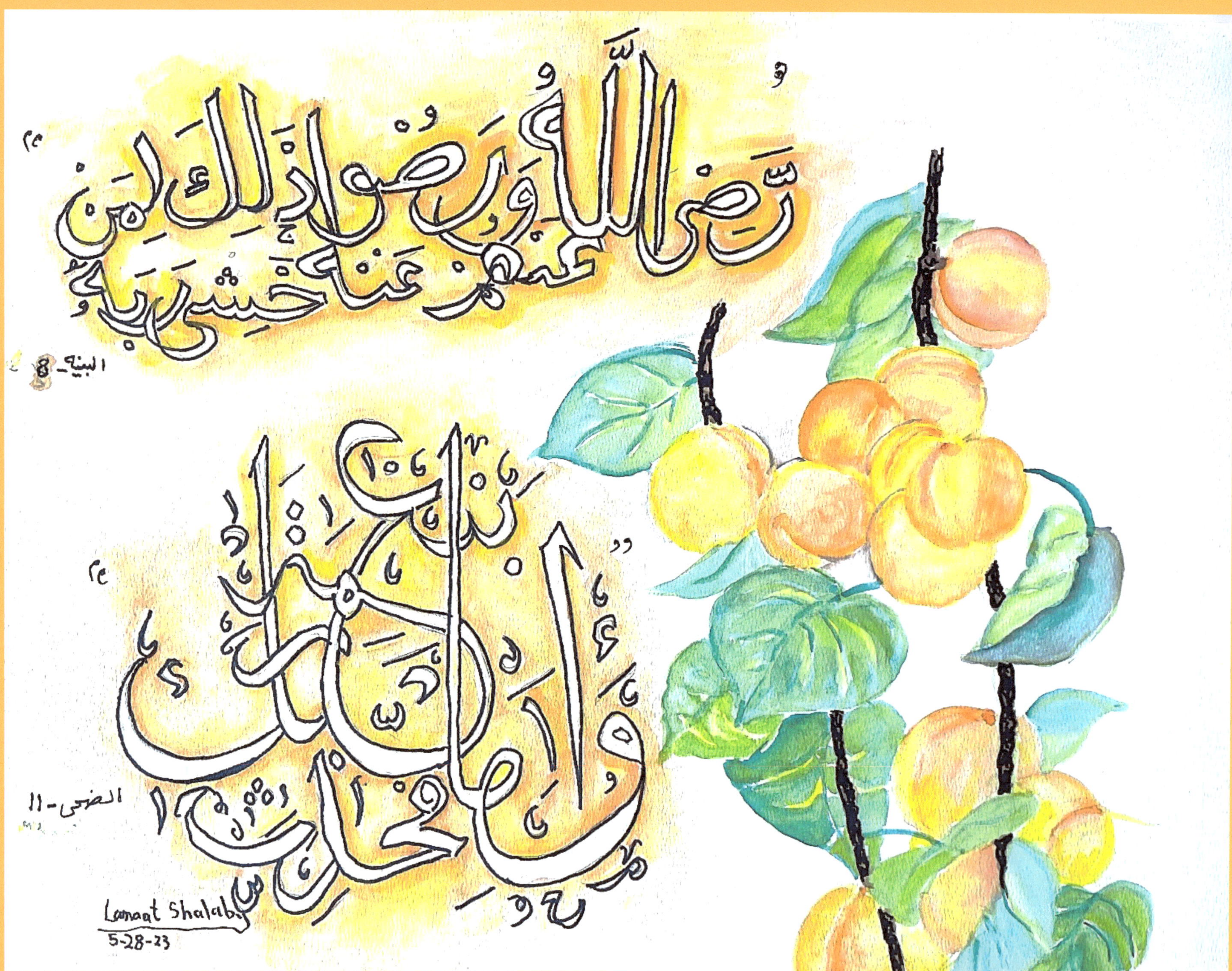
البينة - 8
الضحى - 11
Lenaat Shalabi
5-28-23

Allah's Ridhwan

I looked at a picture of an apricot tree, full of fruit, and said: Glory to Allah. It is so beautiful.
Allah, glory to Him, created every fruit unique in color, shape, taste, texture, and smell.

I felt so grateful to Allah the One and Only God, the Creator and the Most Giving.
What a great reward Allah promised those who believe in Him and the Message of Islam and live by it. The reward is dwelling forever in Jannah
and a fulfilling blessing from Him.

....

Qur'anic Verses in the Painting:

{ Truly, those who believe and do good works are the best of creatures. (7) God has a reward in store for them: Gardens of eternity, through
which rivers flow; they will dwell therein forever. God is well pleased with them and they are well pleased with Him. Thus shall the God-fearing
be rewarded. (8) } Al-Bayyina-7&8

{ Therefore do not treat the orphan with harshness, (9) and do not chide the one who asks for help; (10) but proclaim the blessings of your Lord.
(11) } Adh-Dhuha-9-11

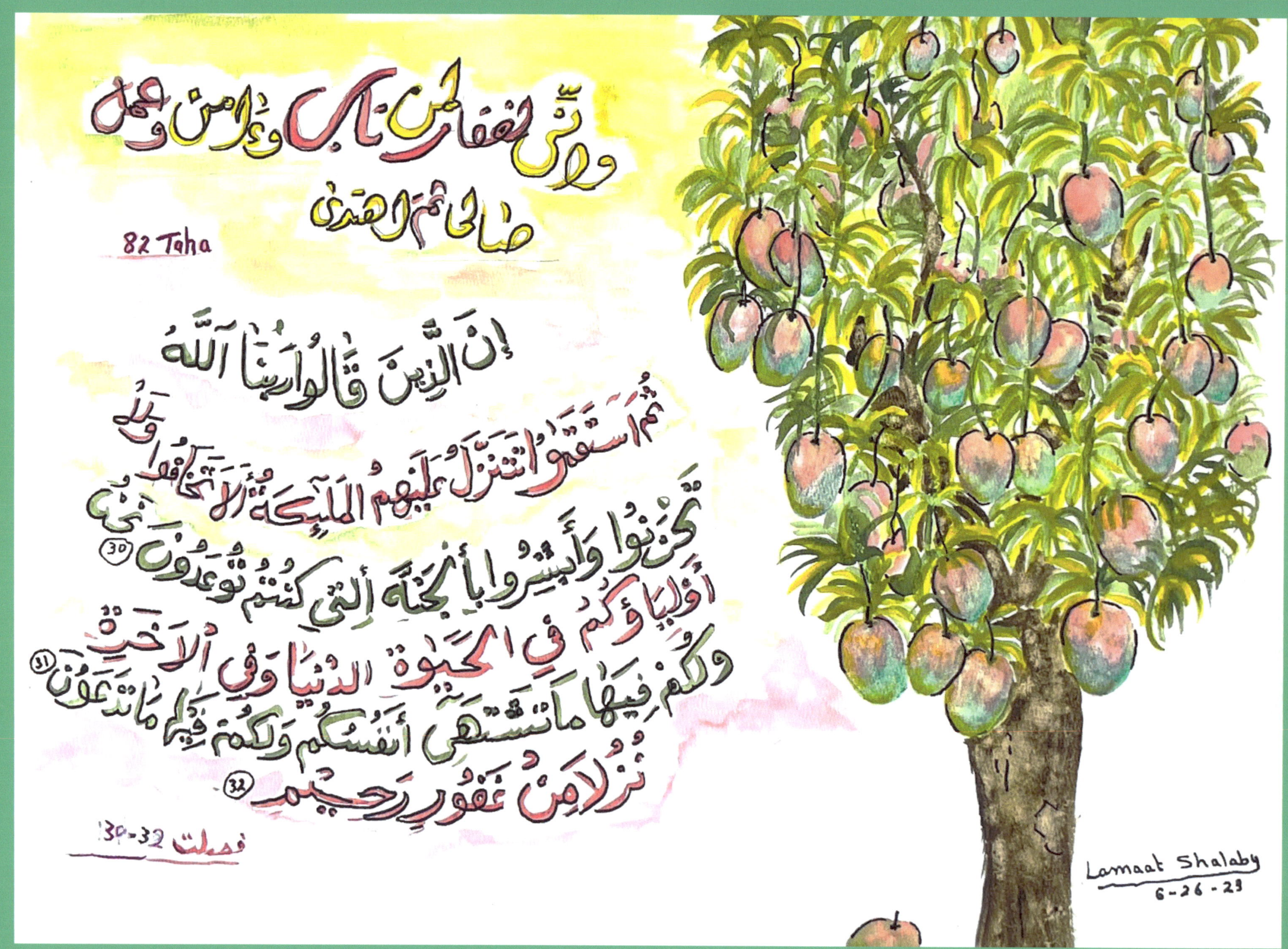

وَإِنِّى لَغَفَّارٌ لِّمَن تَابَ وَءَامَنَ وَعَمِلَ صَالِحًا ثُمَّ اهْتَدَىٰ
82 Taha

إِنَّ الَّذِينَ قَالُوا رَبُّنَا اللَّهُ ثُمَّ اسْتَقَامُوا تَتَنَزَّلُ عَلَيْهِمُ الْمَلَائِكَةُ أَلَّا تَخَافُوا وَلَا تَحْزَنُوا وَأَبْشِرُوا بِالْجَنَّةِ الَّتِى كُنتُمْ تُوعَدُونَ ۝ نَحْنُ أَوْلِيَاؤُكُمْ فِى الْحَيَوٰةِ الدُّنْيَا وَفِى الْآخِرَةِ وَلَكُمْ فِيهَا مَا تَشْتَهِى أَنفُسُكُمْ وَلَكُمْ فِيهَا مَا تَدَّعُونَ ۝ نُزُلًا مِّنْ غَفُورٍ رَّحِيمٍ ۝

فصلت 30-32:

Lamaat Shalaby
6-26-23

Forgiveness Granted

Allah Ta'ala is the most Merciful and most Forgiving. Allah Almighty promises the sinners that He will forgive them if they repent and believe in Him, the One and Only God, His angels, His books, all Prophets and the Day of Resurrection. The repentant must also do good deeds. If he meets all these conditions, Allah will grant him forgiveness every time he repents in good faith.

As it was said in the Hadith Qudsi:

Anas Bin Malik, may Allah be pleased with him, said that the Messenger of Allah said: Allah Almighty said: (O son of Adam, if you call me and ask me to forgive you for what was from you , I will forgive you. O son of Adam, if your sins reach the sky, then you ask for forgiveness, I will forgive you. O son of Adam, if you come to me with the earth size of sins and you don't associate anything with me, I will grant you as much forgiveness) Narrated by At-Tirmidhi and said: A good hadith.

....

Qur'anic Verses in the Painting:

{ I am truly Most Forgiving to whoever repents, believes, and does good, then persists on true guidance." } Ta-Ha-82

{ Surely those who say, "Our Lord is Allah," and then remain steadfast, the angels descend upon them, saying, "Do not fear, nor grieve. Rather, rejoice in 'the good news of' Paradise, which you have been promised. (30) We are your supporters in this worldly life and in the Hereafter. There you will have whatever your souls desire, and there you will have whatever you ask for: (31) an accommodation from the All-Forgiving, Most Merciful Lord." (32) } Fussilat-30-32

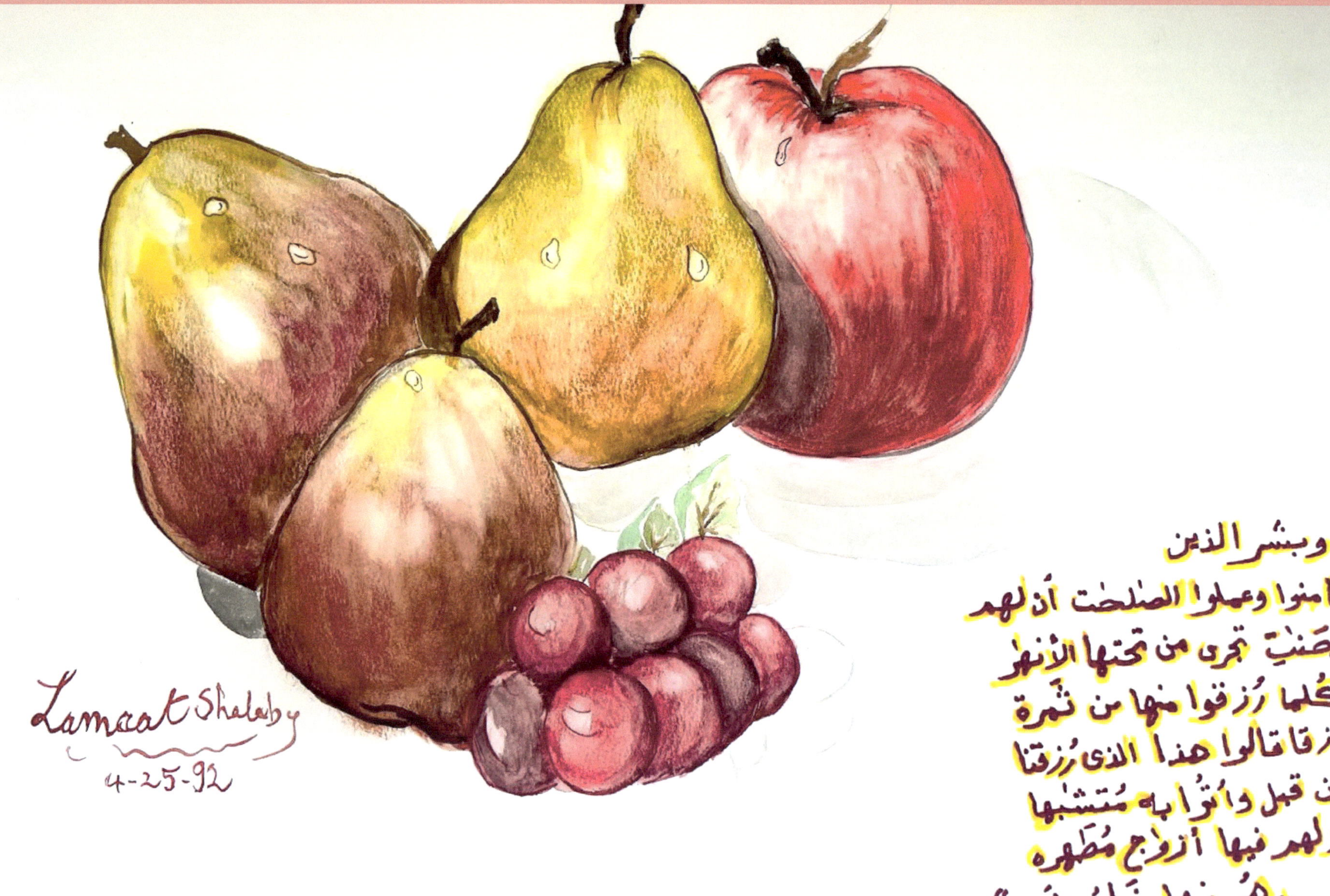

" وبشر الذين
ءامنوا وعملوا الصلحت أن لهم
جنت تجري من تحتها الأنهر
كلما رزقوا منها من ثمرة
رزقا قالوا هذا الذي رزقنا
من قبل وأتوا به متشبها
ولهم فيها أزوج مطهره
وهم فيها خلدون "

البقرة - 25

Fruits of Heaven

When I read verse 25 from Surah Al-Baqara, where Allah Almighty reminds the believers of Jannah and the many bounties they have. It is a pleasure that the fruit of Jannah are similar to the fruits on Earth. This way it will be familiar to us and we will accept it and enjoy it. Glory be to You, my Lord.

{ Give good news O Prophet to those who believe and do good that they will have Gardens under which rivers flow. Whenever provided with fruit, they will say, "This is what we were given before," for they will be served fruit that looks similar. They will have pure spouses, and they will be there forever. (25) } Al-Baqara-25

When I read this, I always remember pears and apples, and all of them are blessings from Allah (SWT) upon us.

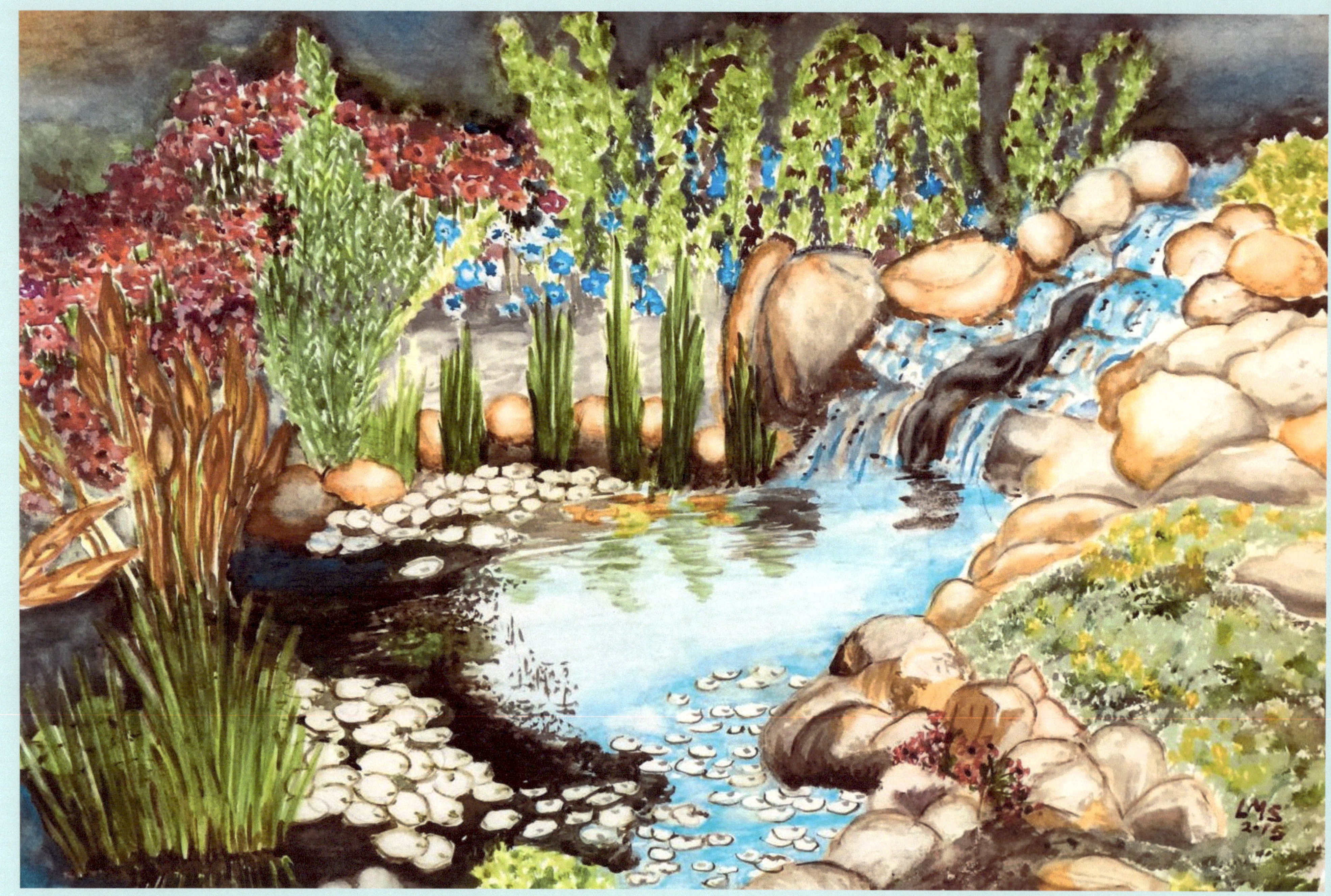

The Gardens of Jannah

I painted this painting at a time when I needed more Noor (Enlightenment) to revive my soul.

I closed my eyes and thought of the gardens of Jannah as described in the Qur'an. There are four descriptions of gardens mentioned in the Qur'an: Gardens of Eden, Al- Ferdous (Gardens of Paradise), Al-Na'eem (Gardens of Bliss), and Al-Ma'awa (Gardens of Refuge).

{ They shall enter the eternal Gardens of Eden, along with the righteous from among their fathers, wives and descendants. From every gate the angels will come to them, } Ar-Ra'd-23

{ Indeed, those who believe and do good will have the Gardens of Paradise as an accommodation, } Al-Kahf-107

{ Those who believe and do good deeds will be guided by their Lord because of their faith. Rivers shall flow at their feet in the Gardens of Bliss. } Yunus-9

{ Those who believe and do good deeds shall be lodged in the Gardens of Refuge as a reward for what they have done. } As-Sajda-19

Thinking of Jannah you will feel Peace, you will hear the trickling water, you will smell the scents of flowers and see the reflection of beauty everywhere and imagine the Angels' prayers. And best of all - being embraced with Allah's Noor and Compassion.

In the two consecutive Surahs: Surah Ar-Rahman and Surah Al-Waqi'a, there are multiple verses about Allah's miraculous creations. Both of these Surahs tell us in detail about the life of pleasure of the people of Jannah compared to the life of the people of the Hellfire. What a frightening difference. The two Surahs complement and confirm each other. For those who want to know more about life of the people of Jannah and those of Hellfire, they can also review Surah Al-A'raf and Surah Al-Hadid.

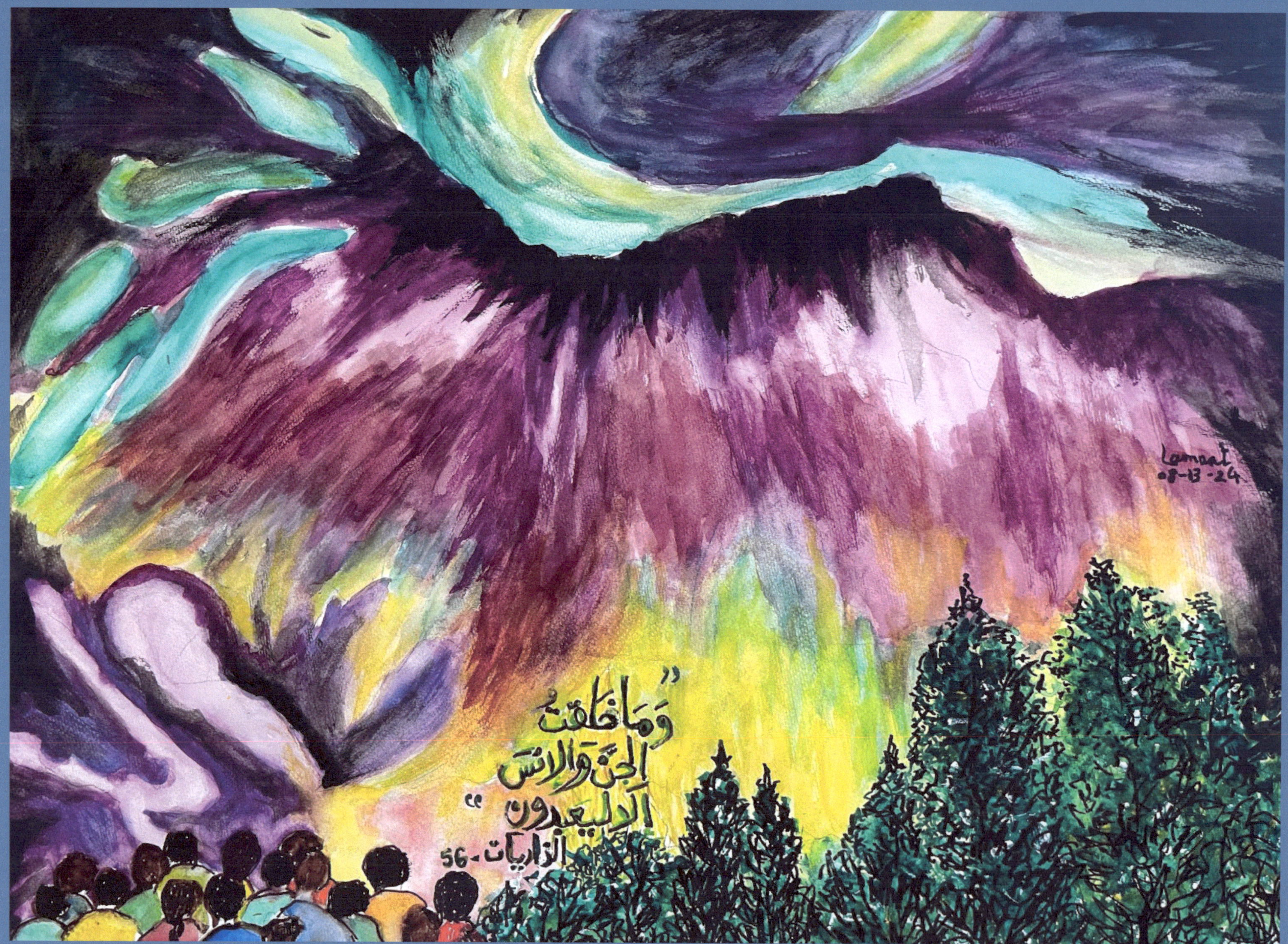

" وَمَا خَلَقْتُ
الجنّ والانس
الّا ليعبدون "
الزاريات ٥٦

The Trust

I am always thinking of the huge responsibility that Allah Ta'ala granted us (The Trust). Mankind has to choose with his free will to follow the way to the Noor of Allah or to sink down to the darkness of evil and the Hellfire.

{ We offered the Trust to the heavens and the earth and the mountains, but they refused to bear it, because they were afraid of it. But man bore it: he surely proved unjust and ignorant. } Al-Ahzab -72

Allah Almighty offered the responsibility of free choice to the heavens, the earth, and the mountains, and they refused to bear it and were afraid of it, but mankind (pledged) to bear it, for he was unjust and ignorant. The entire universe and mankind himself are a testimony to Allah's miraculous creations and how great is the wisdom of His creation. Glory be to You, my Lord, You are the All-Powerful.

Contemplating the miracles of Allah Almighty's creations reminds me of one of them. I remember one day I was on the plane to Canberra, Australia, on a business trip. I looked out the window at night and saw green lights shining in the darkness as if they were flowing. It was a wonderful sight, but I did not realize at that time that what I saw was the southern lights. The beauty and tranquility the northern and southern lights bring to the soul despite the darkness and cold near the poles. Compare this to man-made fireworks, with their noise, potential fires, high cost and air pollution. All of this makes us thank Allah very much for the beauty and perfection of His creation... Glory be to Allah (SWT).
He is the Most Just. I talk to myself when I remember the grace of my Lord and say that He is a Just and a Merciful Lord. We do not bear each other's burdens. After He forgave Adam for his disobedience, He gave us the Earth and its bounties so that every human being could be put to his own test and reap the outcome of his own choices, regardless of whether he is righteous or he is ungrateful.

{ Whoever does a good deed will be repaid tenfold, but those who do a bad deed will only be repaid with its equivalent and they shall not be wronged. } Al-An'aam -160

There are always those warm tears in my heart thinking of Noor Allah, glory be to Him. It could be the feeling of my inadequacy to appreciate Allah's gifts or fear of not doing enough to fulfill Allah's directives. My tears hurt more when I am made aware of someone who is in need or is in pain. O Allah, help me to obey You and fulfill my duties towards You.

....

Qur'anic Verses in the Painting:

{ I did not create jinn and humans except to worship Me. } Adh-Dhariyat-56

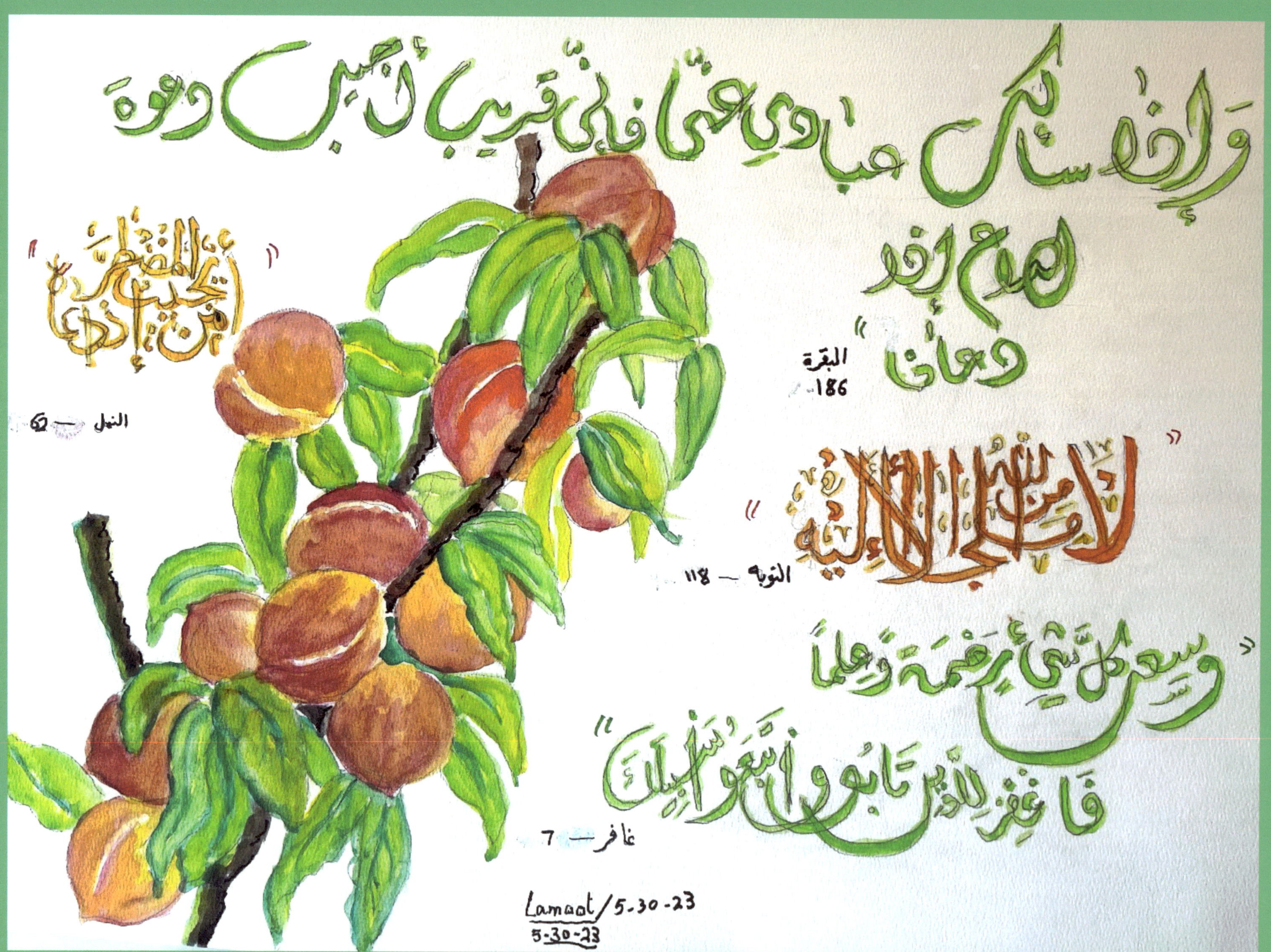

وإذا سألك عبادي عني فإني قريب أجيب دعوة الداع إذا دعان
البقرة ١٨٦
لا إله إلا هو
التوبة ١١٨
وسعت كل شيء رحمة وعلماً فاغفر للذين تابوا واتبعوا سبيلك
غافر ٧
النمل
Lamaat / 5-30-23
5-30-23

No Refuge but His

The peach tree is another beautiful example of Allah's creations for us to enjoy.

In the coming verses, Allah, glory to Him, encourages us to ask for His bounties and to enjoy His mercy. There is no refuge but His.

....

Qur'anic Verses in the Painting:

{ And Allah has also turned in mercy to the three who had remained behind, whose guilt distressed them until the earth, despite its vastness, seemed to close in on them, and their souls were torn in anguish. They knew there was no refuge from Allah except in Him. Then He turned to them in mercy so that they might repent. Surely Allah alone is the Acceptor of Repentance, Most Merciful. } At-Tawba-118

{ When My servants ask you O Prophet about Me: I am truly near. I respond to one's prayer when they call upon Me. So let them respond with obedience to Me and believe in Me, perhaps they will be guided to the Right Way. } Al-Baqara-186

{ Those angels who carry the Throne and those around it glorify the praises of their Lord, have faith in Him, and seek forgiveness for the believers, praying: "Our Lord! You encompass everything in Your mercy and knowledge. So forgive those who repent and follow Your Way, and protect them from the torment of the Hellfire. } Ghafir-7

{ Or ask them, "Who responds to the distressed when they cry to Him, relieving their suffering, and Who makes you successors in the earth? Is it another god besides Allah? Yet you are hardly mindful!" } An-Naml-62

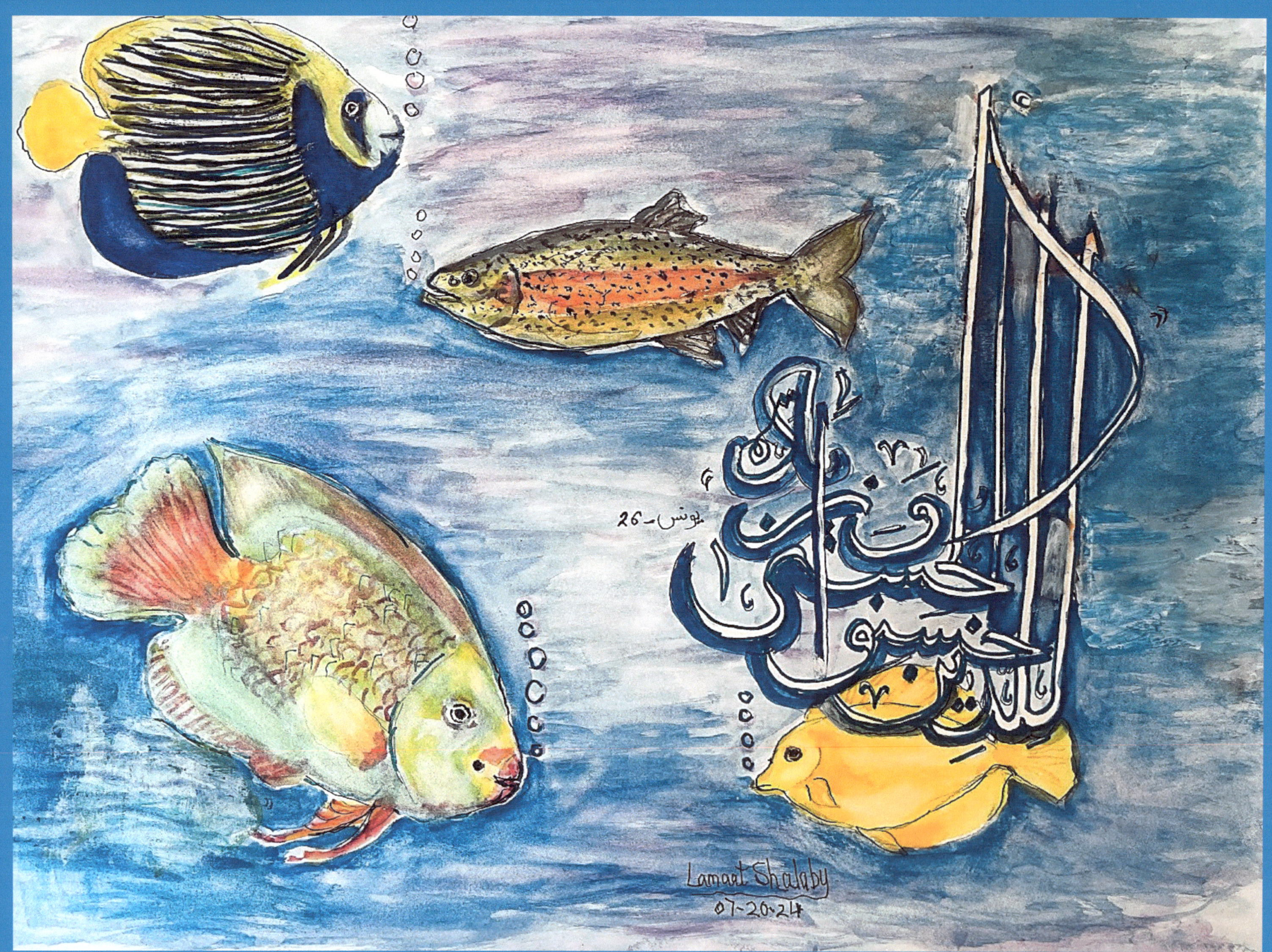
يونس - ٢٦
Lamaat Shalaby
07-20-24

The Ultimate Reward

This is one of the special verses in the Qur'an. It can shake any heart and fill it with joy and certainty. Allah Almighty promises the believer if he is good in worshiping the Creator, and treats people kindly and does good, that he will have "the best". He will have Jannah with all its goodness and an extra reward, which is looking at Him and winning His satisfaction. This is the highest reward and what the believers ask of Him.
I pray that Allah (SWT) gives me this extra reward. O Most Merciful, we always long for You and seek Your satisfaction, glory be to You.

....

Other Qur'anic Verses in the Painting:

{ So be patient with your Lord's decree, for you are truly under Our watchful Eyes. And glorify the praises of your Lord when you rise. }

At-Tur-48

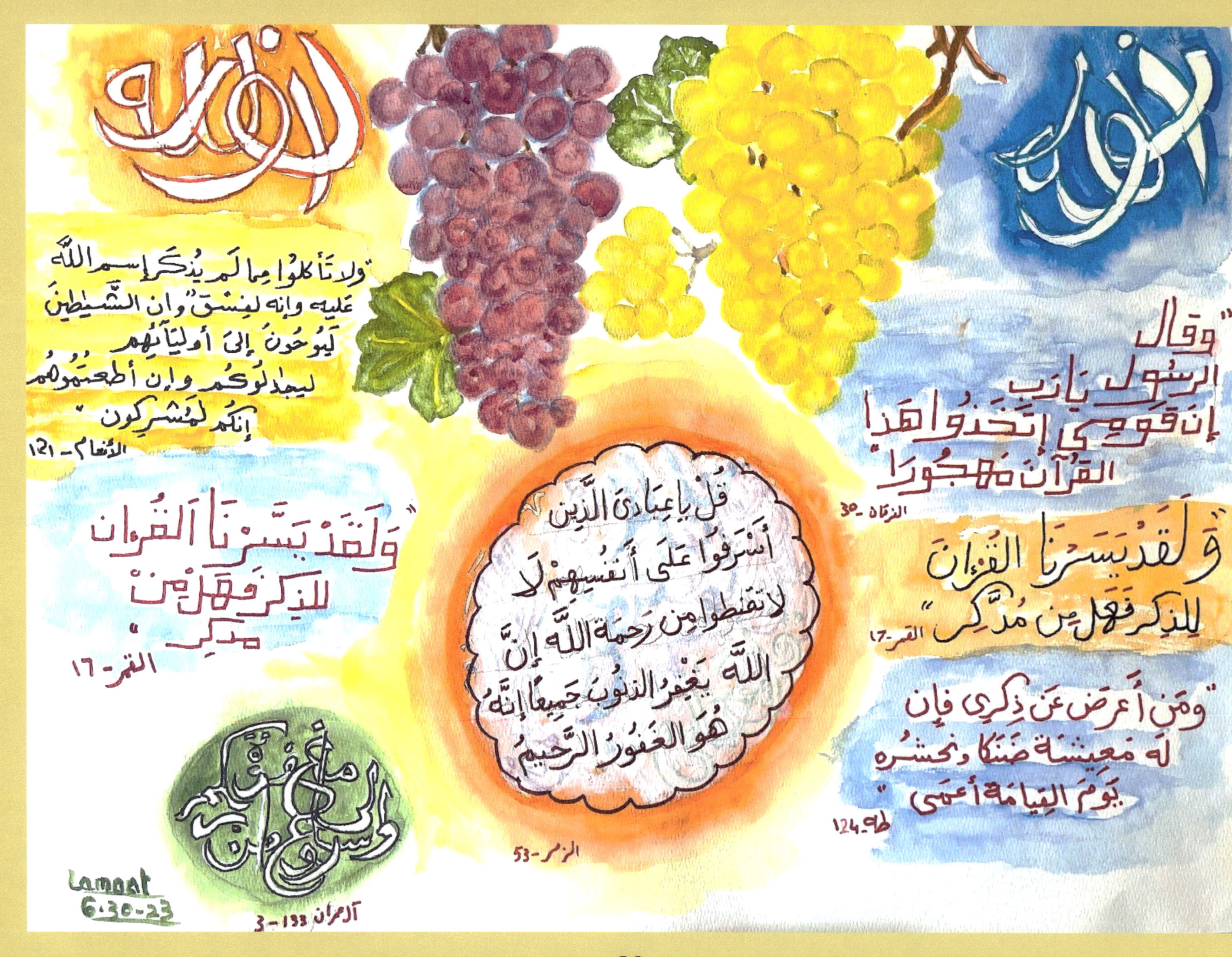

"ولا تأكلوا مما لم يذكر اسم الله عليه وإنه لفسق" وإن الشياطين ليوحون إلى أوليائهم ليجادلوكم وإن أطعتموهم إنكم لمشركون"
الأنعام ٢ - ١٢١

"وقال الرسول يا رب إن قومي اتخذوا هذا القرآن مهجورا"
الفرقان - ٣٠

"ولقد يسرنا القرآن للذكر فهل من مدكر"
القمر - ١٦

"ولقد يسرنا القرآن للذكر فهل من مدكر"
القمر - ١٧

قل يا عبادي الذين أسرفوا على أنفسهم لا تقنطوا من رحمة الله إن الله يغفر الذنوب جميعا إنه هو الغفور الرحيم
الزمر - ٥٣

"ومن أعرض عن ذكري فإن له معيشة ضنكا ونحشره يوم القيامة أعمى"
طه - ١٢٤

آل عمران ٣ - ١٣٣

Lamaat
6-30-23

Where Are The Book Reciters?

What a warning when the Prophet (may Allah's peace and blessings be upon him) complains to Allah (SWT) that his people have abandoned the Qur'an.

I look around and see copies of the Qur'an in houses everywhere and worn by Muslim women as an ornament, but do they read the book or study it? No, most of them are busy with their life and entertainment and are oblivious to reciting the Qur'an. Allah Almighty told us in Surah Al-Qamar verse 17 that he made the Qur'an easy to recite so we can remember Allah Almighty, but many are not reciting it.

{ And We have certainly made the Qur'an easy to remember. So is there anyone who will be mindful? } Al-Qamar-17

Allah Almighty warned mankind in Surah Ta-Haa verse 124 that whoever is straying from Allah's guidance, he will live a challenging life, and on the Day of Resurrection, he will be blind.

{ Whoever turns away from My reminder, will lead a straitened existence and on the Day of Judgement We shall raise him up blind } Ta-Ha-124

In Surah Az-Zukhruf verse 36, Allah Almighty tells us about His punishment for those who turn away from remembering Him. He said that whoever turns away from remembering Him will be disappointed and will never be happy. The Most Merciful will appoint for him a devil that will accompany him and push him to the sinful way.

{ As for one who turns away from the remembrance of the Gracious God, We appoint for him a devil, who will become his intimate companion. } Az-Zukhruf-36

In Surah Az-Zumar-53, Allah, the most Forgiving and most Merciful, addresses those who have committed a lot of sins and despair of Allah's mercy to not despair of His mercy and urges them to rush to ask for His forgiveness, Glory be to Allah, The Merciful.

{ Say, [God says] "O My servants, who have committed excesses against their own souls, do not despair of God's mercy, for God surely forgives all sins. He is truly the Most Forgiving, the Most Merciful. } Az-Zumar-53

Mankind's injustice to himself and his ignorance of Allah Almighty's wisdom in His creation has made him forget that Allah does not need the Qur'an's recitation for Himself. Mankind is the one in desperate need of reciting the Qur'an and understanding it because it will save him from Hellfire and earn him immortality in Jannah. I wish we can all remember this and be among the listeners.

....

Other Qur'anic Verses in the Painting:

{ The Messenger will say, "Lord, my people did indeed discard the Qur'an," } Al-Furqan-30

{ And hasten towards forgiveness from your Lord and a Paradise as vast as the heavens and the earth, prepared for those mindful of Allah. } Al-'Imran-133

CONCLUSION

Allah is The Most Just and The Wisest. Glory be to Him.

At the end of this book, I would like to share with you the most important message that I learned and memorized in my heart. It stays with me always: it is the words of Allah, the One and Only.

{ And [know that] We have not created the heavens and the earth and all that is between them in mere idle play: } Al-Anbiya'-16

{ I did not create jinn and humans except to worship Me. } Adh-Dhariyat- 56

{ He who has created death as well as life, so that He might put you to a test [and thus show] which of you is best in conduct, and [make you realize that] He alone is almighty, truly forgiving } Al-Mulk-2

{ Do people think once they say, "We believe," that they will be left without being put to the test? } Al-'Ankaboot-2

The essence of the message from Allah (SWT) is that we were created to worship Him and that we are on Earth for a certain time to be tested in preparation for the life of immortality, either in heaven with Allah's mercy or in hell for what we have earned.

We have been given the responsibility, which is the freedom of choice in belief and action, and that Allah, Glory be to Him, has made available for us everything in the Universe to believe in His grace, to preserve it, and to enjoy it all. The fate of every human being is in his own hands and it is his choice. Allah Almighty, with His Generosity, revealed the Book to lead us to the path of success and told us that His Mercy embraces everything. If we make a mistake, then we repent in good faith, and Allah is Forgiving and Most Merciful.

The source of evil for mankind is his ego, his overambitious nature, and the whisper of Shaytan. We have to resist these sources of evil through the remembrance of Allah Almighty.

{ But continue to remind. For certainly reminding benefits the believers. } Adh-Dhariyat-55

- Lamaat Shalaby

....

REFERENCES

Ref.1 English translation of the Holy Qur'an:

Qur'an Explorer (online) : Dr. Mustafa-Khattab, Wahiduddin-Khan, Mohammad-Assad and Yusuf-Ali.

Ref. 2 Thomas R. Verny M.D.

Explorations of the Mind.

The Significance of the Heart-Brain Connection

Inside the secrets of the heart. [February, 2022]

Ref.3 Dennis Overbye

"Cosmos Controversy: The Universe Is Expanding, but How Fast?".

The New York Times. [February, 2017]

Ref.4 The Bible, The Qur'an and Science

"La Bible, le Coran et la Science"

The Holy Scriptures Examined In The Light Of Modern Knowledge By Dr. Maurice Bucaille

Translated from French By Alastair D. Pannell and the author.

Ref.5 The importance of bees to humans, the planet, and food supplies

Medically reviewed by Debra Rose Wilson, Ph.D., MSN, R.N., IBCLC, AHN-BC, CHT — Written by Helen Millar

[May 18, 2021]

Ref 6 Which Direction Should a Beehive for Best Pollination?

Science-backed Articles by Jane Ten, Bee Conservationist and Researcher

latest bee answers to questions from learnbees site database.

GLOSSARY

Allah ------ Arabic for God   ---- الله

(SWT) ------ Subhanahu Wa Ta'ala (in Arabic) ------- Glory to Him, The Almighty (in reference to God) ----- سبحانه و تعالى

The Qur'an -------- The Holy Book for Muslims ----- القرآن

Surah ------ Chapter of the Qur'an ------ سورة

Ayah ----- A verse (part of a Surah) ------ آية

(PBUH) ----- Peace Be Upon Him (in reference to prophets) ------ عليه السلام

Hadith ------- Prophet Muhammad's (PBUH) saying ----- حديث

Hadith Qudsi ----- A Hadith in which Prophet Muhammad said that Allah says so and so ---------- حديث قدسي

Wudu ------ Washing before prayers for Muslims --------- وضوء

Salat ----- daily prayer for Muslims (Muslims pray five times a day) ------- صلاة

Al Hajj --------- Pilgrimage --------- الحج

Noor ------ Light (enlightenment) ------ نور

....

Order of Surah in the Qur'an	Name of Surah in English	Name of Surah in Arabic
1	Al-Fatiha (The Opening)	الفاتحة
2	Al-Baqara (The Cow)	البقرة
3	Al-'Imran (Family of Imran)	آل عمران
4	An-Nisaa' (The Women)	النساء
5	Al-Ma'eda (The Table Spread)	المائدة
6	Al-An'am (The Cattle)	الأنعام
7	Al-A'raf (The Heights)	الأعراف
8	Al-Anfal (The Spoils Of War)	الأنفال
9	At-Tawba (The Repentance)	التوبة
10	Yunus (Prophet Jonah)	يونس
11	Hud (Prophet Hud)	هود
13	Ar-Ra'd (Thunder)	الرعد
15	Al-Hijr (The Rocky Tract)	الحِجر
16	An-Nahl (The Bee)	النحل
17	Al-Israa' (The Night Journey)	الإسراء
18	Al-Kahf (The Cave)	الكهف
19	Maryam (Mary)	مريم
20	Ta-Ha (Ta-Ha)	طه

Order of Surah in the Qur'an	Name of Surah in English	Name of Surah in Arabic
21	Al-Anbiya' (The Prophets)	الأنبياء
22	Al-Hajj (The Pilgrimage)	الحج
23	Al-Mu'menoon (The Believers)	المؤمنون
24	An-Noor (The Light)	النور
25	Al-Furqan (The Criterion)	الفرقان
27	An-Naml (The Ants)	النمل
28	Al-Qasas (The Stories)	القصص
31	Luqman (Luqman)	لُقمان
32	As-Sajda (The Prostration)	السَجدَة
33	Al-Ahzab (The Coalition)	الأحزاب
35	Fatir (Originator)	فاطِر
36	Ya-Seen (Yaseen)	يَس
39	Az-Zumar (The Successive Groups)	الزُمر
40	Ghafir (The Forgiver)	غافر
41	Fussilat (Explained In Detail)	فُصّلَت
42	Ash-Shura (The Consultation)	الشُورى
43	Az-Zukhruf (The Ornaments)	الزخرف
47	Muhammad (Muhammad)	مُحمد

Order of Surah in the Qur'an	Name of Surah in English	Name of Surah in Arabic
48	Al-Fath (The Victory)	الفتح
49	Al-Hujraat (The Private Chambers)	الحُجرات
50	Qaf (The Letter Qaf)	ق
51	Adh-Dhariyat (The Scatterers)	الذاريات
52	At-Tur (The Mountain)	الطور
53	An-Najm (The Star)	النَجم
54	Al-Qamar (The Moon)	القمر
55	Ar-Rahman (The Beneficent)	الرحمن
56	Al-Waqi'a (The Inevitable)	الواقعة
57	Al-Hadid (The Iron)	الحديد
59	Al-Hashr (The Exile)	الحَشر
65	At-Talaq (Divorce)	الطلاق
68	Al-Qalam (The Pen)	القلم
71	Nuh (Prophet Noah)	نوح
75	Al-Qiyama (The Resurrection)	القيامة
76	Al-Insan (The Human)	الإنسان
80	'Abasa (He Frowned)	عَبَسَ
82	Al-Infitar (The Splitting Asunder)	الإنفطار

Order of Surah in the Qur'an	Name of Surah in English	Name of Surah in Arabic
83	Al-Mutaffifin (The Defrauding)	المُطَففين
90	Al-Balad (The City)	البلد
91	Ash-Shams (The Sun)	الشَمس
93	Adh-Dhuha (The Early Hours)	الضُحى
94	Ash-Sharh (The Opening Up)	الشَرح
95	At-Tin (The Fig)	التين
96	Al-'Alaq (The Clot)	العَلق
98	Al-Bayyina (The Clear Evidence)	البينة
102	At-Takathur (Vying For Increase)	التكاثر
107	Al-Ma'un (Act Of Kindness)	الماعون
108	Al-Kauther (The Abundance)	الكوثر
114	An-Nas (The Mankind)	الناس